True Magic

Unleashing Your Inner Witch

True Magic

Unleashing Your Inner Witch

Cyndi Brannen

MOON BOOKS

Winchester, UK
Washington, USA

JOHN HUNT PUBLISHING

First published by Moon Books, 2019
Moon Books is an imprint of John Hunt Publishing Ltd., No. 3 East Street, Alresford
Hampshire SO24 9EE, UK
office@jhpbooks.com
www.johnhuntpublishing.com
www.moon-books.com

For distributor details and how to order please visit the 'Ordering' section on our website.

Text copyright: Cyndi Brannen 2018

ISBN: 978 1 78904 243 6
978 1 78904 244 3 (ebook)
Library of Congress Control Number: 2018955408

A CIP catalogue record for this book is available from the British Library.

Design: Stuart Davies

UK: Printed and bound by CPI Group (UK) Ltd, Croydon, CR0 4YY
US: Printed and bound by Thomson-Shore, 7300 West Joy Road, Dexter, MI 48130

We operate a distinctive and ethical publishing philosophy in all areas of our business, from our global network of authors to production and worldwide distribution.

Contents

Do you hear the voice
Of your Inner Witch?
It is a call to rebirth,
To returning,
To renewal.
It is the call of True Magic.

I am
Fire that burns,
Air that breathes,
Water that pours,
Earth that grounds,
And spirit that soars.
I am
Feelings,
Actions,
Thoughts.
I am the watery depths of the Under World,
The starry heights of the Upper World,
And all points in between.
I am
Eternal,
Strong and wise,
Powerful beyond measure.
Sovereign. Free. True.
Witch.
I am.

True Magic

We live on a planet held together by invisible forces,
Circling a giant ball of fire that gives us life,
And beside a moon that controls the sea...
But you don't believe in magic?

You probably wouldn't be reading this book if you didn't feel the call of your Inner Witch. That's the part of you that KNOWS magic is real. There are unseen forces at work inside of us and all around us. Magical thinking is what we need to get beyond what the world has tried to tell us. True Magic is everywhere. It's the Inner Witch inside of us yearning to get out. Unleashing your Inner Witch using the practices in this book will set you on the path of creating your magical life and living your boldest truth. Are you ready? I believe you are.

Finding True Magic

How do you find it? This book will activate the True Magic that is already inside of you. It's there, longing to be unleashed. Set yourself free! Your Inner Witch is all about the hustle. Witches do. Witches go. Witches learn. Witches fight for what they believe in. The activities in this book will get you busy unleashing your Inner Witch. Exercises focus on skills development while the practice activities are about applying these techniques. The journaling prompts are there to guide you with processing what you're learning. Write as much or as little as you need to complete any exercise, journal prompt, etc. Feel free to use point form, charts, tables, bulleted lists, or long paragraphs – whatever works for you. Your Inner Witch has much to do and no time for nonsense.

I carefully selected the various techniques, practices, products and correspondences that are used. I provide substitutions for the botanicals and stones in each chapter in case you don't have access to the ones recommended. True Magic is all about using what's available to activate the immense power of your Inner Witch, so feel free to follow your intuition when it comes to crafting spells and developing your own rituals beyond what I specifically suggest. This book gives you the tools to activate your Inner Witch and all you need to know to practice True Magic. Maybe I'm simply reminding her. I suspect that's the case.

Seven is Magic

We have seven ways in which we relate to ourselves, the world and the mysteries. These categories overlap with each other in many ways. Seven is True Magic.

Seven as a magic number is found across magical traditions and mystical paths. True Magic combines the best of diverse esoteric, mystical, occult and spiritual perspectives to help you unleash your Inner Witch into SEVEN STEPS OF POWER. The seven energetic centers are explored using the chakra framework. The seven Hermetic principles are incorporated as are concepts from Theosophy. From our contemporary time, the concepts of Reiki find their place in our affirmations work. There are elements from ancient mystical traditions, particularly Ancient Greece. All these things combine to make True Magic.

The Septagram

The seven-rayed star is a symbol of enlightenment and metaphysical concepts found in many different paths. It's our symbol for True Magic. In Ancient Greece, this star was linked to the "seven wandering stars" which we now refer to as planets. In each of the steps, a different planetary energy is explored. You'll also work with the points of the star as they correspond to different herbs, stones and other correspondences. In addition, the seven rays represent the amalgamation of the four directions and the three dominions.

True Magic: Seven Steps for Unleashing Your Inner Witch

One of my favorite books is Elizabeth Gilbert's *Big Magic*. I love how she outlines that creativity is magic. Inspiration = creativity = magic = truth. This is what True Magic is all about. Going beyond what *Big Magic* said by giving you the ability to unleash your Inner Witch through the practices and techniques in the following pages. Creativity is connection to all that's within you and all that's without. We unleash our Inner Witch by exploring the Seven Principles of True Magic.

I love a Witch's Ladder. This is really what this book, a ladder of seven steps leading to unleashing your truth and creating an amazing life. Here's a bit about each one of the steps ahead:

#1: Healing

We've got to start at the beginning. That Inner Witch of yours knows what you need to finally let go of all that useless baggage you're carrying around. Trust me, I know how this feels. I dragged around way more than I could carry for decades. I finally just sat it all down. Let me tell you, it took a lot to let it go. You'll get rid of all the toxicity from past hurts and trauma using rituals and other forms of magic in the first chapter. Feel. Deal. Heal. Be real. Be true. Be you. That's the beginning of True Magic.

#2: Relationships

Some of the things we need to heal are way in the past (thankfully), but others are very much in the present. Troubled relationships undergo cleansing, your witches' word get strengthened and you learn all about everyday and magical boundaries in the second chapter. You'll be casting a circle. That's the home of True Magic.

#3: Sovereignty

Sovereignty is such a buzz word these days. Deservedly so. Being independent of what others think and do is what True Magic is. We get into the magic of sigils and magical oils and explore the seven ancient principles of magic in this chapter. Your Inner Witch is smiling already.

#4: Growth

We witch use spells to get what we desire. It's that simple. Now that your inner witch is activated, it's time to start creating the life you know you deserve. First step? Exploring the concept of growth from our witches' mind to casting The Spell of the Seven Fires.

#5: Connections

It's time to go beyond everyday life into the mystical worlds. In this chapter, you'll use techniques to travel to the liminal realm with your spirit animals. Words of power are revealed to you. The only way to access these forces is by being open to them. True Magic is openness. You'll learn how.

#6: Abundance

That Inner Witch of yours knows that you've been selling yourself short. Now that you're standing in your true witch power, you'll realize that the false self, or the shadow, has been holding you back and keeping your Inner Witch prisoner. The shadow healed, you are ready to manifest your prosperous magical life.

#7: Wholeness

One of my personal mantras is "we are not meant to be perfect, we are meant to be whole." Thanks to the wise Jane Fonda for that perfect morsel. In the last chapter, we get into the meaning of unity through more mystical adventures and beyond. True

Magic travels to the heights of The Starry Road. At the end of this chapter you can perform a powerful initiation ritual to fully activate your Inner Witch. True Magic.

The steps in this book are designed to get you busy doing magic. The basic concepts and techniques are discussed at the beginning of each chapter, and then it's onto the practice side of magic. True Magic is about working with natural energies and supernatural forces to effect real change in our lives. *Although True Magic doesn't explicitly include deities and other entities, feel free to incorporate the ones that you work with.* Think of these steps as a framework for understanding and practice rather than rules and regulations.

What is Witchcraft?

Before we get into talking about your Inner Witch, I want to go over what witchcraft is.

Witchcraft is so many things. A way of life. An outlook. An aesthetic. A practice. Some people call it their religion, though I don't. It's perfectly fine if you do. This book isn't about that, though. This witchcraft is about letting your Inner Witch, really your True Self, out. We do this through tried and true methods of witchery. Here are some of the key characteristics of this type of witchcraft.

#1: Witchcraft is Transformation

Witchcraft bends what's available to its purposes. I use what's on hand in my spells, rituals and other workings. Throughout this book, you'll find all sorts of workings – the activities of magic – that use different ingredients and objects to transform them into something greater that will in turn help you unleash your Inner Witch.

True Magic requires transforming things to suit our purposes. Witchcraft is about transforming things - botanicals, stones, objects and energies are examples - to help us obtain a desired outcome. Witches do not merely collect cool things, we transform them into something that suits our needs. Oils, tonics, potions, sigils, talismans, charms, and spells.

Witchcraft is about personal transformation. Yes, I seek to transform the ingredients in a spell for my purposes, but what I am really doing is changing myself. I use all the tools available from personal development strategies to found objects to help create my magical life.

Transforming ourselves and the things we use requires a great deal of will: *So speak I and it is so.* Without that willpower, we can't transform much of anything.

#2: Witchcraft is Adaptation

True Magic adapts to the requirements of a situation or desired outcome. Your Inner Witch knows when to lean into something and when to let it change her. It used to be that witches were marginalized except when their skills became necessary. Not so much these days. Another thing that was true once upon a time was that only women were witches. Men were something else (sorcerers, magicians, warlocks, cunning folk) that was usually far more acceptable. Witchcraft changes with societal norms. Or do we change them? Beats me. One thing that is clear is that this is the Season of the Witch. Writ large and in your life. The time has come to unleash your Inner Witch.

Because witchcraft is so adaptable, there is no need for expensive ingredients or elaborate rituals. While these things can be lovely, witches do what they can with what they have to create what they want. This is why this book is chock full of techniques and practices that are True Magic.

My personal witchery is a mélange of historical and contemporary practices and traditions. I often turn to Old Time Witchcraft for inspiration. My training covers a variety of areas from herbalism to shamanism. I adapt - or apply - what I learn into crafting my version of witchcraft. So many of you do the same. Learning techniques and practices is all well and good, but what's the point if they can't be used to solve our problems? My motto is "better living through witchcraft." That happens through adaptation. Being able to adapt ingredients and ourselves requires the ability to apply our knowledge. Witchcraft requires both information and wisdom. It is a living practice of knowledge accumulation.

#3: Witchcraft is Active

We practice witchcraft. For me, this includes (but is definitely not limited to): burning things, growing things, making things and finding things. Beyond this, witchcraft has other active characteristics: observation, contemplation, exploration, creation and destruction. This is how I find True Magic and I am blessed to be sharing it with you.

Witchcraft isn't something that's done once in a while. It's a way of being in the world. Daily practice in a myriad of forms including meditation, study, witch-crafting (making magical things) and everything that strengthens our witch power is a necessity. I think we all do a lot more of what can be classified as witchcraft than we realize. Witchcraft is all about the doing. However it is you do it, whether in a few stolen moments during your busy day or in wide open spaces.

#4: Witchcraft is Messy

My witchery gets under my nails. It's the pocket full of rocks and plants I always seem to have. My witchery includes blood, bone and botanicals. None of which are particularly clean. There is so much magic in getting dirty and sweaty. That's True Magic. Part of the messiness of witchcraft is that is it intensely emotional. We experience ecstasy and agony through our rituals and practices. Often, we turn to spells in order to alleviate emotional distress. Finally, witchcraft requires emotional courage that is often messy and sometimes risky.

#5: Witchcraft is Risky

There's part of me that welcomes the current acceptance of witchcraft, but a deeper part cries out in protest. Witchcraft has always been on the margins of society, at the edge of the wild. Here in this liminal space, there was great freedom because the threat of confinement was always nearby. Our witch ancestors were of the wild in their connections to animals and plants, and the necessity of making the most of what they had on hand. I think that the wild and free witchcraft of days gone by is not nostalgic, but absolutely necessary.

Witchcraft requires risk. It always has and always should. If what you're doing is completely safe, then it's not witchcraft. By risk I mean you are pushing yourself beyond your previous abilities, you are learning and stepping out of your comfort zone. You are passionate about life and witchery. Not that you drink aconite or bang on drums in your apartment building. Risk is not stupidity. I've designed the steps in this book – tested out by my students over the years – to help you take "two steps to the left." I've heard countless testimonials that these practices help to unleash the Inner Witch.

#6: Witchcraft is Power

Sovereignty is having a zeitgeist moment in witchcraft today. Everyone is talking about personal power. What's really going on is our rebel cry to claim all that we are and are capable of. Lean into this. You are far more powerful than you've ever dreamed. That's witchcraft speaking. The one thing I know for sure is that witchcraft makes us powerful. We have options available to us that others don't. The power is inherently risky, especially for women (at least traditionally). By unleashing your Inner Witch you are standing in your witch power. This is a mighty act of reclamation. Drawing all your power back to you. True Magic.

All this power is completely pointless and very dangerous if it is not filtered through self-discipline. One of the few things I know for sure is that effective witchcraft is only possible with constant self-control. The risk must be balanced with the discipline. The passion finds equilibrium through integrity. Silence is part of this power. I keep silent about what I keep silent about. There are many activities ahead that will help you increase your personal discipline. True Magic requires the balance of control and freedom.

#7: Witchcraft is Personal

Some people will tell you witches must be deeply connected to the natural world. Others will say you need to have a degree (or several) to earn the title of "witch." Then there are those who define the strength of their witchcraft based on the size of their essential oil collection. Witchcraft is whatever you believe it to be. This is where you'll find your personal True Magic. I've spent years honing the content of True Magic, but I want you to adapt the practices how you feel led. The seven steps are core constructs that every witch needs to understand. How you apply them is entirely up to you. It's a balance of learning and intuition. That's True Magic.

Your Inner Witch

A group of women are dancing naked under the blue moon. The night is warm. Energy is buzzing from the heady mixture of the ocean, wine, the moon and the residual magic from their ritual. They run into the sea. Individually they are about as different as a group of people can possibly be. Collectively, they are the same. Free spirits. Healers. Believers. Witches. Since you're here with me now, you know that you have an Inner Witch longing for this sweet freedom. This is the truth of who you are. It's your True Magic.

"We are the flow, we are the ebb. We are the weavers, we are the web."

As healers, witches also hold the power of destruction in their hands. I was taught that a witch cannot heal if they cannot hex. The two are opposite applications of the same energy. And that's all there is - energy. No debates over white, black or grey. There's a problem to be fixed. Witchcraft can help.

The Power of a Witch's Mind

True Magic is about unleashing your Inner Witch. The power source for this is our Witch's Mind. It's about magic that is as old as time. Practiced on the shore, in homes and in secret places. Old time witchcraft knew that the most powerful magical tool is the practitioners own mind. That our curiosity, observations and experiences are what makes us powerful witches.

The Wildness of Witchcraft

Unleashing your Inner Witch doesn't stop at mind work. Nope. That wouldn't be witchcraft at all. You need to get out and do magic. When we take risks and go out into the wild we get a taste of freedom that is often lacking in our modern lives. I'm not advocating for cliff jumping (though it is a blast), but for facing our fears and taking what I call "two safe steps to the left." This can be as simple as writing your own spell if that's slightly beyond your comfort level. Revealing your true self to someone you trust is another taste of wildness because you're tapping into your own "naturalness." Or you can get out in nature to forage for spell ingredients (always wear gloves and be responsible). Speaking of gloves, wild witchery for me includes daily work with various botanicals. Because I like to ignore rules, I burned my thumb dead-heading my aconite this morning. Sometimes, I push it a bit too far. BUT, 99.9% of the time my wild ways work out exceptionally well. My advice, besides gloves: do your research, ask for tips, mash it all together and then get into the wild. You have loads of opportunities do get out in the wild during the steps ahead.

What Your Inner Witch Knows
Your Inner Witch is your True Self. You know so much. In a bit, we'll get into why you need to unleash your Inner Witch when we explore the selves and the shadow. For now, I want to talk about everything your Inner Witch knows.

#1: Witches Know They Are Powerful
Many times in my life I have felt disempowered, at least as an initial response. The absolute worst was when my oldest son was randomly a victim of violence that forever changed his life. In the middle of a night in a pediatric ICU ward, my witch's heart broke through my pain, reminding me that I could make the best out of the situation. It wasn't perfect, but we found our way through. I did a lot of magic and mundane work. Mostly, I tried every day to stand in my own power. This permitted me to conquer quite a pack of demons, including financial chaos and the public education system. Eventually, my Inner Witch power conquered so much more. What has your Inner Witch helped you to overcome?

#2: Witches Know They Have the Solution

Closely connected to belief in our power is the knowledge that we have the solution to any problem that lands in our lap. This is heightened when we work to develop our witchery, through practice and effort. Effective witchcraft requires both. Regularly practicing witchery through learning how to manipulate natural energies and focus the mind helps prepare a witch for anything. Learning transmutation or to how to connect with plant spirits is a transferable skill that we can use in solving complex problems. Confidence is a huge part of True Magic. *Witch tip: Faking it until you make it really works. Spend a whole day engaging in radical confidence. Send your doubts packing. Speak your truth (see below). Repeat until being self assured is as comfortable as your favorite sweater.*

3: Witches Choose Their Way Carefully

When faced with a seemingly unsolvable problem ask yourself, because that's your Inner Witch, "what needs to be done?" I have learned to stop myself from immediately reacting. If you curse someone out of rage, it's highly likely that such a volatile spell will end up sticking to you like glue. Exploring the nature of the problem takes time and effort. This may not be an option in a crisis but training our minds to not react out of fear is a skill that transfers even to the most intense, immediate situations. Perhaps the first step might be to cast a spell for not reacting inappropriately to any situation. Sounds weird I know, but I've done it. *How would your Inner Witch choose to proceed with a challenge that you are currently facing?*

4: The Witch Accepts Things "As Is"

The only way to cast spells that work is to practice radical acceptance. This is the voice of experience speaking - I ran in circles for years until I finally stop fighting what had already happened. It's ridiculous when I think about it. Acceptance is the exact opposite of giving up: it's looking the monster right in the eyes. If you don't know what the monster looks like, how are you ever going to slay him? We get into the triumph of acceptance in the Step on healing. What do you accept "as is"?

#5: The Witch Throws Away the Box

Unless, of course, the box is an inventive solution to the problem. Or if you have a hoarding issue like me. You never know when all those boxes will come in handy. Seriously. When confronted with a problem, use that witchy resourcefulness to see alternative solutions. Work at solving the problem rather than obsessing over it. Again, this is mind work that can be developed through practice. Creativity is a skill that can be developed through various activities, mundane and magical. Once your mind gets used to making things, the neural networks that you've established will also work when facing problems. All my time spent making magical things might be fun, but it also creates a mindset towards original thinking. *How do you think outside of the box?*

6: The Witch Gets Specific

Returning to my example about rage-hexing, reciting a general oath of misfortune when you discover that your romantic partner has been sleeping with your best friend will definitely not turn out well. What you can try instead is a very specific spell (once you've calmed down) that they may know the hurt they caused you first hand. A well-developed spell including a great intention, a well-crafted incantation and excellent correspondences may yield just that. There are risks in hexing. All the techniques in the following pages will get you thinking specific. A well-woven spell takes a great deal of planning. Using a spell written by someone else can be effective, but never as powerful as one you create specifically for the task at hand. *True Magic* gives you everything you need to make those amazing spells. *Witch Tip: Spend the day being as specific as possible with your words. How does this change your communication with others?*

#7: The Witch Sees Failure as a Challenge, Not a Defeat

So, you did the fantastic spell to no avail. It happens to us all. I'm not going to get all super spiritual and say things like, "it couldn't have been for your highest good" or "the universe knows what you need." Sometimes that's a load of crap. The night that my oldest son was in the midst of complex emergency surgery, a well-meaning friend said, "All things happen for a reason." I could say I agreed or forgave her eventually, but it would be a lie. Perhaps he would have discovered the guitar without being permanently disfigured and disabled, we'll never know.

It is him I've been thinking about while writing this section. I've had my share of bad mistakes and random shit storms, nothing compares to what's he's been through. He persists. And if you've ever wondered where I get inspired from, now you know.

If you lose your job, a loved one or your health, it's a serious situation. You may quite naturally feel defeated. We all have times that we give into despair. We try to cast good spells and get nowhere. The witch accepts this but knows the time will come to work magic again. *Have there been times when you let a setback stop you from pursuing a dream? What did you learn?*

Radical Transformation

Letting your true witch self out of that self-imposed prison is a time of great personal transformation often accompanied by intense emotions. Radical changes in your thought patterns will occur. You'll become more embodied – prepare for spontaneous outbreaks of kitchen dancing. All this is wonderful, but the transformation process can be demanding. I've taken all the precautions in the steps ahead to ensure that your transformation goes smoothly.

You may already know what it feels like when you are experiencing a spiritual upgrade that's out of control. The main symptoms are: very strong feeling of the heart center being "on fire", headaches, digestive issues, listlessness, sleep disturbance, vivid dreams, inability to concentrate, hypersensitivity to smells and colors, extreme awareness of bodily sensations (e.g., clothes drive you batty) and temperature (always cold/hot), seeing the material world more vividly, visions, dream oracles, trancing out, "head in the clouds", mood swings (sometimes several/ hour), decreased coping skills and a very strong desire to detach from relationships (although this can swing the other way into preoccupied attachment). You can't get grounded or comfortable. Your shoes don't feel right. Your pets look at you funny.

I've been through this. Although unleashing your Inner Witch is powerful, it shouldn't be painful. If you've been through this in the past, you know how horrible it can be. This is why I've designed and tested all the exercises. I know they unleash your Inner Witch without those nasty side effects.

If you've got many of these symptoms already, it's okay. This is why we begin with healing. Before we get into that, I want to talk about some of the big ideas behind True Magic.

The Principles of True Magic

The witch commands the supernatural forces feared by others. Through intention, will and action, we stand sovereign over all things. Using our powerful minds to alter the course of what has already happened and to create magic. Witches rely not on the gods to save us, but we turn to them for support while we save ourselves. We call upon the elements of air, earth, fire and water, enlisting them as our allies. With the moon in our pockets and dirt under our nails, we ride our brooms confidently through life.

The worlds of *form and force* intermingle when you do True Magic. We combine our internal powers with the external energies to manifest our desires. The forces worked with include: the four elements, the three energetic realms, their physical manifestation in the three dominions, the liminal realm, the three selves, and the accompanying three functions (actions, feelings and words). With correspondences, we bridge the two worlds by taking the physical object and pulling out its mystical properties in the various ways we work with the objects. Correspondences merge our internal witchery with the external forces. The ones we use in True Magic include the moon, the elements and the three worlds. Getting to know these potent energy sources is the first part of developing your ultimate witch skills. Always keep in mind that correspondences and other forces support your personal power. No object or external energy is more powerful than you.

Correspondences

I love using correspondences, including plants, stones and colors. To me the process of carefully choosing them for a spell or ritual is True Magic. The better we are at selecting them, the stronger our spells. In each step, there are correspondences specifically chosen based on hundreds of years of Old Time

Witchcraft knowledge. The correspondences include colors, botanicals (herbs, plants and trees), stones and crystals. I've included trees to represent botanicals. Herbal correspondences will be introduced in each step. You can use various parts of any botanical, unless otherwise indicated. You can use bark, branches, essences, flowers, leaves, oils or seeds. In a pinch, a picture will work as well. Another technique is to write the name of the tree on paper. It's the energy of the botanical that matters most. While having the actual tree works best, the other techniques can work just fine. Now is a good time to obtain them so you have them on hand when the time comes to use them.

For healing, you'll need yarrow, ginger and a hunk of obsidian. While, in our relationship work, citrine is the stone and the botanicals are a magical wood like ash, rowan or poplar and sage. Onto the third step where you'll work with amethyst, birch and frankincense. True magic grows with the help of olive, orange and chamomile in addition to red jasper. In the fifth chapter, our step on connecting, blue agate, mugwort and oak are utilized. Abundance is associated with many stones and botanicals, we use three of the most potent ones: aventurine, pine and bay laurel. Finally, wholeness gets added oomph from moonstone, myrrh and elm.

You'll find loads of color magic throughout the book, so it's a good idea to stock up on different markers, pens and colored paper. The colors include: black, yellow, purple, red, blue, green and white.

If you work with the Tarot, I've included recommendations in each chapter as well. Tarot helps unleash your Inner Witch in many ways. A daily Tarot practice of drawing a card or two in the morning for guidance during the day is part of my Witches' Hour of Power. I recommend pulling a card at the beginning of each step for insight into how to best approach the topic. Tarot cards are excellent as energetic enhancements for almost any type of witchery. You can add them to spells as correspondences.

Contemplating and activating the energy of specific cards or even entire suits can be enormously beneficial. At the beginning of each step there are suggested cards for use. Study the cards mentioned, noting their symbolism and your reactions as well as the standard interpretations for your deck. There is a section at the end of this book further outlining how to prepare and use Tarot cards.

Botanicals

There are seven (no surprise there) parts of plants used in True Magic: *seeds, roots, stems, flowers, fruit, bark and spirit.* I chose each of the botanicals because they are all quite easy to access and have diverse purposes. I don't care for super-specific correspondences. I like them to be flexible. The seven chosen can form the basis of your magical apothecary if you don't have one started yet.

All correspondences have two basic types of energy – form and force. Regarding plants, their physical form often contains ingredients that can be used in magic in addition to their mundane applications. Force refers to the energetic qualities of a botanical – its ether. Working purely with plant energy focuses on connecting to the spirit of the plant. There are different forms of the physical plants that we'll work with in our magical endeavours: bark, ground root, essences, oils, seeds and spirit. These will be used with different techniques: making a banishing stone, imagery, making an incense, using smoke, making magical water and making a talisman.

Note: Responsible use of all botanicals is encouraged. Test small quantities before going all out.

Stones

Stones are typically worked with for their energetic properties alone, unless, of course, you need to throw one at someone. That can be a very magical experience! I've selected a stone with properties that reflect each step. All the stones selected are readily available from metaphysical stores and from major online retailers. I recommend a size that is about the size of a silver dollar. If you already have the stones, you can purify them, but I do suggest purchasing new ones. You should have a new/cleansed piece of *clear quartz* on hand, too. It can be used as a substitute for any other stone and is generally just a good thing to have around while doing magic.

Colors

I love color magic so much. I start the day by picking out clothes, well a scarf, because I usually wear all black, that sets the energetic tone for the day ahead. If you're a member of the Keeping Her Keys Community, you may have noticed that I use color magic in many ways. Probably my favorite technique is to use colored inks and papers for various purposes, especially for writing **voces magicae (words of power)** on or **constructing sigils**. Paper is also great for making symbols, like moon phases. If you're a visual artist, drawings and paintings are a fantastic way to conjure energy.

In addition to the seven hues covered in this book, silver and gold (for representing yourself and the divine respectively) are good to have. I love paint pens. A white paint pen is a great tool, as well. Although having paper in the seven colors is a good idea, you can make do with high quality white paper (and black if possible). String in the seven colors, or at least white and black, is another thing you'll need. In the last step, the magical project is creating a talisman using all the colors. This can be accomplished with polymer clay or another similar product. Polymer clay can be painted, so you can use a mix of craft paint with a few different colors of clay to keep costs down.

The Seven Phases of the Moon

The moon's phases are influenced by the position of the earth in relation to the sun. The ensuing shadows give us the experience of each part of the cycle. This, in turn, influences so much on earth, including the tides, crops and our moods. In True Magic, you'll draw down this energy to add power to your rituals and spells. Lunar energy is so intense that we don't even need to overtly connect to it. Simply being aware of the phase and performing witchery that corresponds with it is often enough. Of course, there are so many ways to intentionally tap into lunar magic. The simplest form is to concentrate on the energy of a phase while envisioning capturing it in your hands. Feel the energy and then either pour it in your spell or add your intention and release.

In each step you'll explore the different phases. In True Magic, we work with seven distinct lunar energies:

New Moon: when the first sliver appears in the night sky. About two nights after the astrological new moon (when there is no visible moon). This is the time to harness the energy of the new phase for all types of beginning magic. Use this time to set your intentions for the month ahead and then follow up with additional workings during the most appropriate phase.

Waxing Crescent: about days 4-7 into the cycle. The influence of beginning is still strong but shifts towards pure manifestation energy as the moon returns. Great time for doing all sorts of attraction magic involving beginnings, from starting a new business to finding a new romantic partner.

Half Waxing: Days 7-12. Between the half crescent and the full is the time for massive attraction magic , especially spells involving making what you already have grow.

Full Moon: Day 14. When it comes to the full moon (and the dark), give yourself 24 hours on either side of the exact time to do your magic. Slightly before will lean into attraction magic and after into removal. The full and dark moons are equally powerful for balanced magic consisting of both attraction and removal aspects. You want to remove blocks and open the way. Full moon time is more about illumination while dark is for things hidden.

Half Waning: Days 16-22. Best time for removal magic, like protection and reversals, is when the moon appears to be growing smaller. Closer to the full moon, to make use of the lingering impact of illumination energy.

Waning Crescent: Days 23-27. The pull of the dark moon is heavy on the almost invisible moon. Deep, dark magic happens in this phase.

Dark Moon: Day 28/1. The dark moon is the liminal time between the old and new cycles. This is the phase to turn to for cleansing as the moon will extract harmful energies while it is dark. Also the time for secret workings, sex magic and spirit contact.

Watch out for the moon being "void of course." You can consult a good witchy or occult calendar for this info. When the moon is VOC its energy is not available for making magic.

Drawing Down the Moon

Drawing down the moon is a lot like calling the elements and summoning the energies of The Three Worlds. Envision the energy of the phase, starting by looking at the moon. Then widen that to the moon's influence on the earth around you. Let it seep into your being, synchronizing the energy with your internal forces. Finally, let this combined energy flow into your hands or chosen tool, like the wand or the blade.

Examples of chants:

New moon: *Moon, moon returning tonight, shine on my intentions, bring them to light.*

Waxing moon: *Moon, moon as you grow, take my intention and make it so.*

Full moon: *Moon, moon full and free, I call your energy down to me.*

Waning moon: *Moon, moon as you flee, take my worries away with thee.*

Dark moon: *Moon, moon dark and pure, I call your hidden powers to make my magic sure.*

The Elements
Earth my body,
Water my body,
Air my breath,
Fire my spirit.

The four compass directions and the elements of air, earth, water and fire are the most powerful source of external Earth based energy after that of the moon. In every step, you'll learn how to connect with the elements and use it to unleash your Inner Witch. I love working with the elements. If you're a fan of my blog, you'll already know this. Head over to Keeping Her Keys to find loads of examples in addition to everything in this book.

Characteristics of the Elements

Earth: associated with the north and "earthy" colors like green and brown. Connect to this element in muddy places, the forest, caves and in basements. A downward facing triangle with a line bisecting it is the symbol for earth.

Air: associated with the east and yellow, white and grey. Standing on top of a windy cliff, along the sea-blown shore or at the top of a tall building is where you'll be able to feel the power of this element the strongest. To represent air in your sigils and spells, use an upward triangle with a line through it.

Fire: the direction is south and red, yellow and orange can be used to represent it. The sun and the stars are the ultimate fiery sources of energy, but when it comes to the elements we're sticking to earth-bound fires. Lighting a candle to contemplate the energy of fire is an accessible way to explore this element. The upward pointing triangle is the symbol for fire.

Water: to the west for most of us, although some traditions reverse east/air and west/water. I use water with the west in this book. Ice, snow, lakes, rivers and, of course, the ocean. A downward pointing triangle is the symbol for water.

Working with the Elements

When you are working with the elements, it is good to have such a symbol on hand. For example, you can have the smoke from your incense representing air, the burning incense for fire, a dish of earth and your chalice with water. This helps you to connect with these forces on the macro level. Building your altar to include tools that contain the energy of each of the elements and realms is another way to evoke and honor them. We can connect to these objects as conduits to the large forces. They can also serve as a mediator to make the forces more manageable.

The energy of the elements can also be worked with in spells. When using them in this way, it's important to really contemplate what the element's force is and how you are using it.

Witch Tip: Start to observe the four elements as part of your daily commute or go for a walk exploring how they are represented around your home. The more you study the elements, the easier it will be to make True Magic with them.

The Three Worlds

The elements are the physical energies here on this planet. They have forms from which we draw energy for magic, but there's also three energetic worlds that are also reflected in the Earth's physical and energetic properties. All the elements are situated at the Middle World but branch out towards the other two realms. The elements of earth and water connect to the Under World, the realm of emotional energy. Fire and air stretch to the intellectual Upper World. The elements are active moving energies, such is the world of force at the Middle World. Another way to understand the three realms is by the distinctions of sea, land and sky. The elements reside on the "land" but reach down and up to the two. Adding these energies to the four elements makes our True Magic Seven.

Think of it this way the Middle World represents our everyday lives. It is the realm on which we are having this current human experience. The Upper World is the realm of higher consciousness, the place where our unborn souls eternally reside, while the Under World is the deep dive into the realm of life and death. Under World energy is heavy and dense and that of the Upper World is light and refined. At the depths of the Under World, the experience is overwhelming because we can't see anything. We can't breathe because the air is too heavy. At the heights of the Upper World, we are overwhelmed because we can perceive everything. It's like standing on top of a mountain on a cold, clear day. It's difficult to breathe because the air is so light. Thus, in our human form, we must remain in or near the Middle World, although we can experience brief sojourns into the fringes of the other two realms. But, their depths and heights are not places for humans.

Characteristics of the Three Worlds

Under World: Black is often used to represent the dark and dense emotional energy of the Under World and the Lower Self. The sea and caves are excellent places to do Under World magic. The direction is downward, expressed with your left hand. Roots and seeds are good symbols. Represent the Under World in your sigils and spells with three waves. Stand under the night sky during the Dark Moon to feel the emotional Under World energy, contemplating how all life comes from the darkness of the wet womb.

Middle World: Red is the color of the realm of actions and our Middle Self. Represent the Middle World and Self with the equal armed cross of the compass, signifying that the elements also reside here. The location is the heart center on the body with both hands touching it and each other. Physical locations are crossroads from the joining of roads to the juncture of land, sea and sky. Stand here with your hands at heart center and feel all the elements and worlds meeting.

Upper World: The mystical and intellectual energy of the Upper World and Higher Self is represented by white. To connect to Upper World energy, raise your right arm high waving a feather in a windy, high location on a crisp, sunny day. Stars represent the Upper World, especially the septagram.

Working with the Three Worlds

The Three Worlds are represented by sea, land and sky. The four elements are all placed within the Middle World with connections to the sky through air and to the sea through water. Earth is firmly situated within the Middle World, and fire as its energetic and spiritual energy. Plants are an excellent way to connect with the energy of the Three Worlds. Their roots and seeds represents the Under World, stems the Middle and branches and flowers the Upper. The Under World's emotional energy can be explored through water and underground spaces.

Roads symbolize the action of the Middle World. High places and intellectual spaces like libraries can help us connect to the Upper World. Think of the elements as forces bound to the energy of the planet while the Worlds extend far beyond.

The Liminal Realm

The Liminal Realm is also known as the Other World. It is where the Three Worlds meet in the land of pure force. This is also the energetic home of many deities and entities and is the location of the Dream World and the Astral Plane. In the Three Worlds Animal Spirit Journey you'll be travelling in the Liminal Realm to connect with the other energetic realms to receive personal words of power from three different animal spirits.

Liminal Times

There are liminal times of the day as well, including dawn and twilight.

The Three Selves

The three realms also exist within us. Our external self is the result of the combination of our three internal selves. This is often a façade that we put out there to save ourselves from real or imagined threats to our true self – our Inner Witch. This is the shadow self. When we release our Inner Witch, we tame the shadow. Listening to what others think of us and what they have done to us really can mess us up. We need to heal and manage our past and relationships. The Lower Self is the realm of emotions, while the Middle Self is the land of actions, and the Higher Self is the place of intellect. These three combined make us into the unique creations that we are. Our internal voice is a compilation of the three selves.

Just to make this even trickier is that each self can have a shadow aspect. We can be prone to dark emotions, dysfunctional thoughts or harmful actions. The three often go together, but not always. Here's the final bit: each of the selves has a part of our soul in it, so that our soul is emotional, active and thoughtful. They combine into our unborn or eternal being that goes from incarnation to incarnation, inhabiting a different body with the accompanying personality and experiences. It's all that great universal school of ascension to whatever it is that lies beyond human comprehension. I'm not sure what that is, but I find thinking about the selves, the shadow and the soul very helpful, so this is how I'll talk about them throughout the book.

The Lower Self

While some may perceive that the Under World as a foreboding place, it is deep within our own beings that emotions dwell. You can think of our emotions as roots that extend down into the soil of the Under World pulling up the nutrients necessary to fuel both our actions and our intellect. It is our emotions that can lead us into a destructive version of the Under World – we can be anxious, depressed or suffer from significant distress. We use the metaphor of the "dark night of the soul" to describe difficult times in our lives. The primary sensation associated with these painful experiences can be found in our emotional responses. Thus, the Lower Self is seen as the realm of emotions. The energetic location of the Lower Self is from the pelvis down to the bottom of your feet. This energy extends deep roots down into the earth. We can release our pain into the ground and find rebirth. Through this approach, we can learn to quell our fear-based emotions, healing the shadow and unleashing your Inner Witch.

The Higher Self

At the other end is our intellect, the dominant energy of the Higher Self. If our Lower Self energy gives us roots into the earth, then our Higher Self is our branches reaching up to the heavens. This is the realm of thoughts. Our thoughts are the one part of our Functions that we truly have dominion over. No matter what the situation, we can change our thoughts to better manage what's going on. We can release harmful thought patterns up to the skies above to find healing. Our positive thoughts create a powerful force within ourselves and the world. The Higher Self is in the land of intellect, when we are in control of our destructive thought patterns, we are naturally highly motivated to seek out knowledge and further our personal development. The energetic location for the Higher Self is the crown of our head.

The Middle Self

In between the Lower Self and the Higher Self is the Middle World self. The primary energy of the Middle Self is the action that arises from the combined energies of our intellect and emotions. The energetic core of the Middle Self is at our heart center. Thus, wisdom is gained through the activities of the Middle World self or we hurt others and our behaviors if we are being controlled by our Shadow Self.

The True Self and Shadow

When we are born, we bring with us into this life a self that is true and essential. This self is our combined experience from previous lives, infused in our very DNA. It is who we are. The True Self which for us is our Inner Witch can also be understood as the soul or the Higher Self. The True Self is our connection to the mysteries and to metaphysical forces, including entities and deities. The True Self is the combination of our Three Selves.

However, many of us experience people, ideas, and events that teach us that our True Self is wrong. When we are very young, our brains don't have the capacity to accept when others negatively judge us, but around the age of five we begin to develop the capacity to examine our thoughts and feelings. We develop a sense of self and a concept of "others." If we are validated, then our True Self continues to be the self that we present to the world. When there is invalidation or trauma, the True Self can become hidden, not only from others but from ourselves. Your Inner Witch, aka your True Self, is protected but caged.

A wall can develop around the True Self. Think of this wall as a strategy of self-protection surrounding your Inner Witch. The wall contains all our hurts, fears and pain. This wall is the Shadow Self. The Shadow Self functions in each of the Three Selves. What was whole, meaning the connection between our True Self and the energetic forces, becomes fractured due to the imposition of this barrier by the Shadow Self. We can no longer directly connect to the Divine, the energy source, because of this wall. While we live as our shadow, we often feel empty and distressed. In addition, we can't seem to accomplish the things that are important to us. Practicing True Magic enables you to remove the power of the shadow self and reconnect with your True Self.

The Voice of Others

When we were very young, we acted and spoke as we felt. Sometime around when we started school, we internalized the collection of maladaptive voices of what others thought about us. The Voice of Others is a powerful dictator over our desires, thoughts, and actions. The Voice of Others is directly connected to the Shadow Self, so that when we turn away from one the other begins to weaken. Your Inner Witch doesn't need validation from anyone. Once your Inner Witch is freed, this energy drain will start to magically vanish.

Magical Techniques

All these energies are utilized in various ways throughout the steps ahead. We start out with removal magic and progress onto attraction workings. Then it's onto a purification ritual of deep emotional healing. In the Second Step the power of the magic circle is explored as a mechanism of protection. The type of magic utilized is protection. In Sovereignty, the Third Step, the magical emphasis is on the technique of transmutation with the focus on self-acceptance. In the following Step, a mixed method combining both removal and attraction magic is used to facilitate your understanding of Growth. I am crazy about The Spell of the Seven Fires in that step. So many students have reinforced my personal transformation through this spell. The last three Steps are devoted exclusively to attraction magic. In Connection, the Fifth Step, communication with non-verbal entities is explored, while in Abundance spellwork is applied to fully activate your creation of a meaningful life. Finally, in Wholeness, a full-tilt trip to the Starry Road for rebirth is on board.

Preparing for True Magic

To get your True Magic started, a simple commitment ritual and preparing for the journey ahead is your next step. The place to begin is through creativity, particularly by writing. If you are more of a visual artist, feel free to use this medium as you feel led.

Writing (or voice recording, one of my fave techniques) every day about your problems and successes/disasters in life and witchery creates your own database. Consult your notebooks when a setback occurs to help guide you with a new solution. I refer to mine whenever some new disaster comes calling. In order to keep great records, we need to develop strong observational skills. Start noticing your feelings and the events of your life as they relate to the moon phases, astrological considerations, the weather and other things. We need to correspond these factors to life events. Some of these things go in your True Magic Journal and others belong in your Book of Shadows.

Your True Magic Journal

Start by picking a notebook that's easy to use and durable. I recommend a hard-back spiral bound one, but there are so many options to choose from. Whatever you select, make sure it's easy to carry with you since you'll be keeping it with you during spells and rituals. You might also want to take it everywhere, so you can record your thoughts about the content and the exercises when they come to you. I'm a big believer in keeping journals. You should have a dedicated journal just for True Magic. I'm slightly obsessed with Pinterest and bullet journals. Head there to find inspiration to create your True Magic Journal.

Book of Shadows

A witch's Book of Shadows is their record of their magical workings. There are countless ways to make your Book of Shadows, so I'm not going to get too much into the details about what it should look like. You may already have an established one. If that's the case, then I recommend continuing with it, unless you feel strongly that you need to start fresh. It can be a regular notebook (my usual), a binder or a hand-crafted masterpiece. I use fancy spiral-bound hard cover notebooks. I prefer these – I've used lots of different types – because they are easy to hold onto during workings.

I keep a Book of Shadows that is separate from my personal journal, like your True Magic one. I highly recommend that you do the same because the energy of our personal journals can be quite intense, especially if we are doing deep healing work. We want the energy of the Book of Shadows to be balanced. Furthermore, we want a degree of separation between our innermost thoughts and our Book of Shadows. The journal is your place to let it all out, while the Book of Shadows is a more organized and structured account of your magical workings. Speaking of organization, I like to use the pages with the pockets on them for keeping important reference materials in. I make cards of the lunar phases, important dates, correspondences, etc. My Book of Shadows extends to my laptop where I keep documents, e-books, lists of things and the many databases that I create. A witch's Book of Shadows can be whatever you want it to be. The only thing it needs to be is easy to use in a way that makes sense to you. Techno witchery is modern True Magic.

I usually arrange mine in chronological order, although many others sort theirs using different categories. I use those little stick on tabs to highlight different things. I also use different colored inks to indicate the various topics. It's such a personal creation that I don't want to give too much away about my own approach! Typical contents of a Book of Shadows includes information about deities, prayers, meditations, rituals, magic space, correspondences, herbs, divination work, and spells (of course).

On the first page of your Book of Shadows you can make a cover page with designs, symbols and other magical images. You can draw them or use existing pictures. Be creative. As you construct your title page, concentrate on the intention for your Book. When the title page is finished, I recommend doing a dedication ritual. It's doesn't have to be elaborate. Add a statement of commitment for using the book for the highest good and end with, *"My intention is true, and my will is strong."*

Practicing True Magic

We work with tools in addition to correspondences and the energies when we practice True Magic.

Tools

The tools will be introduced one at a time in each of the seven steps with an emphasis on how it can be used in conjunction with the energies related to the concept.

Bells are used for two purposes – to clear the energy in a space and to get the attention of energetic forces. Use whatever type of bell appeals to you. I have a jingle-bell bracelet like what belly dancers wear. In the first step, we use the *cup* to explore the watery side of the Under World as a tool for personal healing. None of the tools needs to be fancy or expensive. You can use ones you already have, look around the house for potential items or make them. I broke my *witch's blade* and grabbed a knife (a rather nice one) that never was used as a quick replacement. I fell in love with it, made a black handle for it and use it all the time. I use a turkey *feather* from my ancestors' farm with ribbons tied around it to summon the energy of Air, the dominion of Sky and the realm of the Upper World. It's also a representation of my intellect and Higher Self. I have always changed *wands* for different purposes, but some people prefer one that they use for everything. Whatever works for you. A lot of the time, I don't use a wand, but I always have one as part of my magical set up. The offering bowl is for containing energetic representations of the dominions and elements.

I love burning things – from incense to bridges (just kidding). That last part was a joke, sort of. A *censer*, that is a heat-resistant bowl safe for burning incense, small sticks and bits of paper in is one of my favorite magical tools. If you can't or don't like to burn things, you can still place the herbs and other objects in a dish and connect with their energy this way. For the portable altar, you might want to keep the hot censor off it in case the glass is very thin. I had a pentacle one blow up when it got too hot. Explosive magic!

Your Witches' Cupboard

You'll be making things throughout the steps, so some basic witchy equipment is in order. Use what you have on hand, give everything a good scrub before using it for magical purposes. However, you may not want to go back to using a piece of equipment for everyday uses after since some of the botanicals can leave traces. When possible, use glass instead of plastic or metal. There's some debate about the best type of pot metal for magical cookery, but I have found that a well-cleaned stainless one yields great results. If you don't have a mortar and pestle, a hammer and a strong plastic bag can substitute. A tea pot with a built-in strainer is excellent for making tonics and potions.

In addition to the paper, markers, etc. discussed earlier, you'll also need charcoal disks (you can break up BBQ ones or order the ones for burning incense from any major online retailer) and salt (preferable natural sea). Pieces of fabric and small bags are good to have on hand – either in an energy neutral form (like natural burlap) or corresponding with the intention of your working.

I always use a black candle to cleanse the space before starting and to catch nonessential energies in the objects I'm using. It's also good for keeping intrusions at bay. This is a candle that should be prepared (dressed) for maximum effectiveness. There's a note on candle preparation following the object preparation section below. I prefer beeswax candles that I draw or paint the appropriate color or symbol onto, but colored ones are great, too. You can purchase a big box of them from major online retailers quite inexpensively. I keep a 70-foot coil of wicked beeswax on hand that I cut for my purposes. If you can't burn candles, invest in a set of high quality battery-operated votives. You can paint and draw on them.

A black cloth covering your work surface when making magic is an additional way to ensure purity of the objects you're creating.

Preparing Objects for Magical Use

It's important to prepare correspondences and tools before involving them in a working. Basic preparation includes cleansing each object of any existing non-essential energies and consecrating it for magical purposes. This is usually done for tools and most objects like stones, bones, etc. Botanicals are a bit different because we may not want to expose their properties prior to using them. Removing their original packaging – which can contain nonessential energy from having been harvested and otherwise handles – is helpful. Then store them in a clean vessel, like a jar or bag. We cleanse objects to release energies that aren't associated with the specific symbolic powers of the object. For example, if I am using a new crystal in a spell then I want to remove the energy of all the people who have handled it while it made its way to me while keeping its inherent properties. There are a variety of methods for cleansing objects, such as leaving them outside under the Full Moon, placing them in a jar of magical water or smoking them over incense. Salt is a powerful medium for releasing non-essential energies. Try to use natural sea salt. I like using a large shallow container, like a tray to cleanse objects in salt. If you're pressed for space, a zippered bag filled with salt does the job nicely.

The moon can also be used to purify objects. Most objects will be sufficiently cleansed after a few days, especially if you've put them in there during the Full Moon. When you place an object for cleansing, say something like "You are cleansed of all that's past, free to release your magic at last." You'll need to check-in with the salt to determine when it is full of these unwanted energies and then change it. How long this takes really depends on how much non-essential energy that the correspondence objects you've cleansed in the strophalos have.

The second part of object preparation is to consecrate the item for magical use. You'll be able to tell that an object is ready to leave the salt by picking it up. It will feel clean and you'll feel its energy. When this happens, take the object and pass it through the smoke from incense several times. Sage, of course, is a great choice for using for this purpose. I usually do this in multiples of three. You can recite something like this: "I hereby claim this object for my magical workings. My intentions are true, my actions wise and my will is strong." Your object is ready for use as a correspondence.

Candle Preparation

Candles can have their energy removed via salt like other magical objects. In addition, they can be dressed in oils and herbs to infuse them with specific energies. Drawing or painting on them accomplishes a similar goal. To dress a candle, let it rest in the salt for a few days first. Then rub the candle with a magic oil, you can use high quality olive oil like you'll need for the step on growth. In general, you can rub the oil in either clockwise or counter clockwise for attraction or removal magic respectively. Then you can rub a few drops of an essential oil correspondence onto it as well. I often roll the candle in scattered herbs as well. Note to go lightly with the herbs if this is a new technique for you. You don't want to have them catch on fire. If it's an all-purpose candle without a specific use, then letting it rest in salt is what I do. If you're using battery operated candles, you can place them on salt to cleanse them, too and end with, *"My intention is true, and my will is strong."*

True Magic Altar

The altar is often the focal point for magic. This is where we place our tools, position our magical objects, and activate things. It's not at all necessary but it certainly helps. Making a septagram, the seven-rayed star, as the foundation for your altar is a great way to focus your energy starting out. You can draw or paint one on a frame or print one. Creating one out of salt, sand or earth works as well. Tiny stones can be arranged in the shape. It's entirely up to you how you create the septagram for the basis of your altar. Each step you'll be adding a new tool to it.

A portable altar made on a tray or picture frame makes it easy to move around. I love portable altars because I usually change up mine to reflect whatever sort of magic I'm making or to reflect the lunar phase or the season. Altars are an amazing way to express our True Magic through creativity. They are a link between internal and external forces. Not everyone can have a huge altar set up all the time or have little ones everywhere like I do. A portable altar gives you that flexibility. If privacy is your concern, a portable altar is easily placed under the bed (a great magical place to keep it...you'll be able to connect with it whenever you like, and no one can see it) or even a closet. Practicing True Magic doesn't require you to take over the house. Unless you want to. I highly recommend it.

If you can't manage any type of altar, remember that an image, stone or candle is a type of altar if you use it that way. The altar is the bridge between our internal forces and external energies. Cool things are great but not always possible or necessary.

If you can, purchase or make seven candle holders and candles to acknowledge the completion of each step. Having them in the same colors as the ones used in the step will deepen your understanding, so you can draw or paint them to match. The candles used in your septagram altar should only be lit at the competition of each step. Construct a Step Completion Ceremony where you meditate on your achievements of the Step while lighting the corresponding candle and adding the accompanying tool to your altar.

Unleashing Your Inner Witch

We're almost at the seven steps, but before we get into them I want to talk about the most important part of True Magic. The thing that will unleash your Inner Witch, also known as your true self. I think you get that by now. It's the *Witch's Hour of Power*. By dedicating one hour per day to True Magic, you can achieve the meaningful life you seek. The seven magical practices include:

1. Journaling
2. Meditation
3. Knowledge Building
4. Divination
5. Energy Work
6. Creating
7. Ritual

Journaling we've already discussed. I hope you've been making notes. Knowledge building, you're in the thick of it with this book. Divination is about a daily Tarot practice. Pull one card every morning while contemplating your intentions, plans and activities for the day ahead. Energy work is about practicing magic – doing spells, using correspondences and the energies. Creating is what you'll be doing throughout the steps, including making charms, potions and more. Energy work also includes connecting to and using the seven external energies and attuning them with your internal ones. Circle casting is the pinnacle of this sort of energy work. Ritual refers to connecting to your inner energies and external ones without an intention to use these for any sort of purpose, like casting a spell. A daily ritual where you connect with and give thanks for whatever external energy you are currently exploring is a great way to honor your Inner Witch. The daily practice of a ritual and the other parts of the Witches'

Hour of Power reduce the shadows' shade over your true self.

I don't want you thinking that you need to dedicate an entire hour each day. Do the best you can. Write for a few minutes, draw your daily card and try to do the meditation below as often as you can.

The True Magic Meditation

The witch's mind is the most important tool at our disposal. Through our focus, creativity and cleverness we learn to connect with the moon, other forces and correspondences. The Witch's Hour of Power is designed to help you develop your mind for magical purposes. It has the added benefit of helping in everyday life. There are two basic types of meditation. In one, the emphasis is on quieting the mind either through chanting or not. The goal is to practice thought and emotional release. In guided meditation, imagery is used to direct our attention to achieve focus. The True Magic Meditation is in the latter category. It uses the energy of the seven steps to create a state of calm awareness. This state is necessary for any sort of consciousness altering work, like ritual or mystical journeying. It's also the optimal state for most of life. You can incorporate it into your daily practice. I've provided the text below, and you can listen to the audio of it with the link provided in the email for this section.

A note about this meditation: if you are familiar with the chakras, you may have noticed that the colors don't exactly line up with the usual ones. However, the energetic properties of the definitions of each chakra can be applied to the steps even when the color associated differs.

Our Magical Hands

I use hand positions and gestures in witchcraft quite a bit. As such, this meditation involves different ones for each of the energy centers. I use the term "mudras" to describe these positions, borrowing them from chakra meditation techniques.

We can attune these energy centers by chanting specific sounds. In general, your breath should be deep and slow. The sounds, if you're saying them, are said on the exhale. Move your hands in sequence with the matching text section of the meditation. Mudras are specific hand positions that activate corresponding energy centers in the body, mind and spirit. The sounds and mudras augment the power of the meditation and helps train you on how to use your hands and voice to influence your personal energy by connecting to external energy currents since each position connects to a corresponding one – both within and without.

Hand Positions for this Meditation

GENERAL HAND POSITION: Place your hands on your lap. Face down or up, your choice.

SPECIFIC MUDRA POSITION for each area:

HEALING: hands together, fingers crossed with index fingers extended. Both hands toward ground (sound: LAM) concentrate on the lower body.

ENERGY: left hand under the right, hands in your lap, palms up, tips of thumbs touch (sound: VAM). Concentrate on the base of the spine.

SOVEREIGNTY: Hands on belly in prayer with fingers pointing away from you. Fingers touch, thumbs are crossed. (sound: RAM) …Concentrate on the area between the belly button and the solar plexus.

GROWTH: left hand down towards the ground, right one faces up. (sound: YAM). Concentrate on the physical area around your heart

CONNECTION: Cross your fingers on the inside, let thumbs touch each other to make a circle. Place near throat if comfortable. (sound: HAM). Concentrate on your shoulders and throat.

ABUNDANCE: Hands in front of the solar plexus. Wrists

meet to form a "V" with your two hands. Thumbs touching towards heart. (sound: OM). Concentrate on the area above your eyebrows, but below hairline connecting down to your fingertips.

WHOLENESS: Cross all fingers, left thumb under the right. Point index fingers up, like the steeple of a church. Hold as high as comfortable.

The True Magic Meditation Script

The goal of this meditation is to create unity with what is below, what is within, what is without, and what is above.

Sit comfortably, with none of your energies crossed (i.e., ankles, arms, legs, eyes). Sit straight, feel the length of your spine. Don't be stiff, though. Relaxed but strong.

Before beginning check in with your breath. Breathe as you normally do, but notice that breath…where does it stop? In your chest, belly, back? Just notice it for now. Now we will begin the journey of unification. Slowly count from 1 to 13. As you count you will begin to become more and more relaxed. Place your hands in the resting position.

Count 1: The healing breath is felt in the throat and can often be heard. Breathe in through your nose. As you breathe in, feel the breath as it moves down your throat. In the throat let the breath expand so that it makes a soft noise (according to the specific mudra if a specific stage is being enacted).

Now, as you continue to count your breath will move deeper and wider…

COUNT UP FROM 1 – 13, WITH EACH NUMBER BRING YOUR BREATH (Your back is expanding on the in-breath, with shoulders widening).

Now that your healing breath is fully activated, we will begin the journey towards unification. *Move your hands in the healing position.*

Turn your attention to your feet. Envision the floor beneath them, travel, in your mind's eye, down through the floor, down through the foundation, right into the ground beneath. Feel the coolness of the ground. Let your feel become attached to the ground, feel roots descend out of your feet into the ground. Feel the strength of those roots. The roots are a solid black, beautifully releasing and nourishing. They flow from the lowest part of your torso, down thru your legs. Allow all the fears and pain you have seep down your roots into the ground. The Under World needs your destructive energies for they are part of the cycle of life that sustains us all. As the destructive energies are drained, feel the beneficial energies come up through your roots.

YOU ARE NOW GROUNDED BELOW.

Move your hands into the energy position.

Turn your attention to the base of your spine. Imagine a beautiful bright ball of sun energy filling this area. It is nourished by the roots and any destructive energies herein travel down thru them to be released. The sun begins to fill your body burning away hurts associated with relationships.

Move your hands into the sovereignty position

Now your travel to the area just above your belly button this is the centre of the energy of the self. Purple is the color for we are sovereign beings, ruling over ourselves. The color of royalty. Allow the regal power of your Inner Witch to flow from this center, creating self-love and confidence. Releasing your true self.

Move your hands into the growth position.

Moving onto your heart centre, feel the glowing red of our internal fire in this energetic center of the action. All missteps of the past are released, replaced by fiery energy born of the true self.

Feel the unity of these four areas of your body. They are now in harmony. You have created the energetic state perfect for personal growth.

AND YOU ARE NOW UNIFIED WITHIN.

Move your hands into the connection position.

Next you travel up to our throat which is coated in beautiful blue. It is through our thoughts and words that we connect with others, with objects through reading. So much connection happens through our communication center. Release and bring in as you feel led to. Feel the harmony. Now, without opening your eyes, see other people doing the same meditation elsewhere. Visualize a connection spreading from person to person. Expand this connection to your physical surroundings let the energy pour out of you as you absorb it. Let this go even further to your community. See the world as one huge connected web with you in the middle. You are strong in this position, protected from others' harm, sharing your true self safely.

YOU ARE NOW UNIFIED WITHOUT.

Move your hands into the abundance position.

Here you visualize all the energy within you and without intermingling, merging together in your hands. You feel energized, grateful, whole.

Move your hands into the unity position.

Here you are connected to the Upper World, the heavens or the starry road. Whatever you prefer. This is the realm of intellect, wisdom and psychic gifts. Allow the cord between you and these talents to open. Feel the pull of the Upper World, the desire for wisdom and understanding coming down from above like little stars replacing distress and tension with curiosity and creativity.

You are now unified ABOVE.

Stay here for as long as you need to. Feel the state of unification, within, without, above and below. When you are ready, pull up the cord into the earth below. Zip up the red root energy centre deep in your torso. Zip up your energy centers, moving up each one...closing them, but being aware that you can access that energy at any time of your choosing...thank them for their energy...

As within, so without.

As above, so below.

It is from this place of unity, of perfect love and pure trust, that we achieve the state of calm awareness.

Take a few moments to bask in the unity...below...within... without...above.

Now we will start to return to this place and begin our work.

Count down from 12...on each breath bring yourself back into your physical body...refocus your attention to your body, your surroundings, the others in the room...while the unity we created remains...resist any chatter that starts to come into your head...refuse any tension in your body that tries to return...

I recommend journaling about this experience, especially the first time you do it. When we connect to the energy centers like this, messages can come up, emotions can be released. You may feel very energized or quite tired. After the meditation, you may feel sleepy or very energetic. If you are sleepy, it may be because you released excessive emotions and need to rest while the balance is restored. If you are energized, you could have been "too much in your head" and released a lot of excess thoughts. As the three selves are now unified, in a state of balance, you may feel like focusing on one aspect more than another. This is especially true if one of the three selves had been neglected. Pay attention to how you feel, think, and act in the days that follow. Writing about them in your journal is a good idea. You can do this meditation whenever you feel overwhelmed, stressed or too wound up to help return yourself to a balanced state.

Unleashing Your Inner Witch Ritual

It's time to begin. Any ritual is an extension of an intention. Indeed, all magic is based on the notion that the intention is the most important part of any working. Perhaps you are already familiar with this idea. Setting intentions is a vital part of magic, so it's fitting that you begin your journey with True Magic setting a great one. In this simple ritual, you'll activate your intention for unleashing your Inner Witch.

NOTE: *The ultimate lunar energy to use for this ritual is that of the Full Moon because you are releasing the chains around your Inner Witch while simultaneously activating your powerful True Magic by connecting with the elements and worlds.*

Guidelines for Writing Intentions

A strong intention needs to be very specific and use as few words as possible. An intention is a way of summarizing our desired outcome. By going through the process of thinking about what we hope to achieve, we can narrow our focus to exactly what we want. The more precise an intention, the more effective the spell. Broad spells that ask for generic things are likely to fail because there is too much ambiguity. The clearer we are with our intention, the more likely we are to use energy to our advantage. The best example of how an imprecise spell can lead to undesirable results comes from a student of mine. She desperately wanted a position as a veterinary assistant, so she did a spell to manifest a job working with cats. She got a job alright – working at a discount store with a giant tiger for its logo! Her desire did not match her magical intention. Don't let this happen to you.

In addition to their magical proficiency, specific intentions help to activate our behaviors, thoughts, and emotions towards manifesting our desired outcome. We'll be motivated to do all we can to manifest our goal. Thus, a great intention brings into alignment our magic, actions, feelings, and thoughts. With this powerful combination, how can our spells fail?

Steps for Developing a Great Intention

- Write down all your initial ideas using a word web. What does unleashing your Inner Witch mean to you?

- Once you've got them all down, study them for common themes. Connect the themes using lines or circles. Whatever makes sense to you.
- Next, use these common themes to identify the main intention. Be as precise as possible. Be very specific and use as few words as possible. Write your intention on the work sheet.
- Copy your intention on a separate piece of paper. You may want to write your intention on a piece of durable paper since you'll be posting it somewhere to remind you that you have unleashed your true self. If you're so inclined, you can use decorative paper or decorate a plain sheet using symbols important to you, especially the seven-rayed star. While I'm making the symbols, I concentrate on my intention and develop the words for the rituals and make an action plan.

Once you've written your intention, it's time to do the unleashing ritual. For this ritual, you'll need a candle of some sort, preferably white. It's fine if its battery operated – not everyone can have an open flame in their homes. You can print the seven-rayed star at the end of this chapter or make your own. You'll also need a single sheet of paper to write your intention on. If you work with Spirit, you can have representations of the elements, entities or correspondences that are meaningful to you as well.

Requirements
- Your intention written on a single sheet of paper
- White candle
- Your septagram image or altar

Directions
- Wash up before beginning.
- Set your candle, intention, and star near each other in a

clean space. Place the candle in the center of the septagram if possible.

Incantation

- Light the candle. Say, "I light this candle to unleash my Inner Witch."
- Envision the Seven-Rayed Star growing so that it surrounds you. Three points represent the Land, Sea and Sky and your Three Selves. Four points represent the directions and elements. As you say each line of the incantation, see the star being filled with the energy of your intention.
- While holding your intention in both hands, hold it towards the sky and say, "Sky above, may my intellect work to unleash my Inner Witch, my true self and my power." Now point your hands towards the ground and say, "Sea below, may my emotions unleash my Inner Witch, my true self and my power." Finally, hold your hands over your heart center and say, "Land on which I stand, may my actions work to unleash my Inner Witch, my true self and my power." You have completed the first three points of the star.
- Call upon the directions and the elements to strengthen your intention. You can use a compass app on your phone to find them.
  - Turn to the North and say, "Energy of the North and Element of Earth, may my roots of truth and power be deep."
  - To the East: "Energy of the East and Element of Air, may your winds blow away all that stands between me and my true self and power."
  - To the South: "Energy of the South and Element of Fire, may you fan the flames of my truth and power."
  - To the West: "Energy of the West and Element of Water, clear the way for my truth and power."

- You have completed the final four points of the star.
- Now turn to the star and read your personal intention near the flame, saying, "I release this intention into the energy of the Seven-Rayed Star, may you guide my thoughts, feelings, and actions so that I manifest my truth and power."
- Pause for a few moments so you can contemplate your intention being released into the star. Feel the energy of the worlds and elements merging with you, activating and unleashing your truth and power. You may receive a message at this point. If one does come forward, make sure you write about the experience in your journal.
- Once you complete releasing your intention, release the elements, directions and realms. Begin with the last energy summoned – in this case it's water. Visualize the energy of your energy being sent out into the world as each of the points is released. Say for each of the seven points:
  - To the West and the Element of Water, Hail and Farewell.
  - To the South and the Element of Fire, Hail and Farewell.
  - To the East and the Element of Air, Hail and Farewell.
  - To the North and the Element of Earth, Hail and Farewell.
  - To the Land, Hail and Farewell.
  - To the Sky, Hail and Farewell.
  - To the Sea, Hail and Farewell.
- Write about your experience during this ritual in your journal.
- Keep the intention in a spot where you'll see it several times a day – like on your bedroom mirror or bulletin board near your workspace.
- *You can adapt this ritual for any type of manifestation work.*

Being an Ethical Witch

Having firm boundaries is a vital part of developing an ethical practice. We get into boundaries in the step on relationships. Before that begins, I want to briefly touch on being an ethical witch. You've just unleashed your truth and power. You may be full of energy and eager to use it. Take it slowly. If you are feeling too much power, release it into the ground beneath you. There are practices ahead that will help you learn to manage your unleashed capabilities. Another thing that may occur is the urge to help others. When you do decide to help someone else, you must consider the implications. While it's a great idea to do witchery for someone else, make sure you do so with the intention of helping them achieve their highest good. Don't do spells involving another person unless they ask you or consented, except when there is a real danger to yourself or others.

Ethical practice extends to how we represent ourselves in the world. Specifically, when we are talking to others about our practice, we shouldn't try to convert them to our way of thinking nor should we belittle their beliefs. However, there are times when another person's belief or behaviors represent a significant risk to their own health or that of others. In such cases, it may be necessary to get involved.

While the ethics of healing may be easy to comprehend, the actual process of applying witchery to another can be very complex. I encourage you to take training in energetic healing methods, such as Reiki. You can also take courses on herbalism and crystal therapy. Developing your empath or psychic skills through formal training or structured self-study is another part of ethical practice. The steps ahead focus on your own power and shouldn't be considered preparation for healing others.

Healing

Acceptance is the absolute first step in any magical working. We need to put our energy into solving a problem rather than resisting its existence. When we do this, we clear the path for developing intentions that will lead to the outcomes we desire. Resistance is like spiritual or energetic dirt. We need to be purified from it through acceptance.

Starting this Step

Here we are at the very beginning of your journey with the Seven Steps. You've done your unleashing ritual and set up your altar. Now it's time to get down to the business of going up the steps. We start with healing. Why? There's no other place to begin. That's where we tame our shadows, releasing their hold over our Inner Witch. At the start of each step, you'll find a section on the energies and correspondences of each one, so you can plan and purchase what you need. It drives me a bit bonkers digging through a book to find the ingredients I need to do a ritual. I didn't want to do that to you.

Waning Moon

Healing can involve any part of the lunar phase, but I'm emphasizing REMOVAL magic in this Step. You're going to take away all that's holding you back.

Energies

Healing is emotional work first and foremost, so the energy of your Lower Self and the Under World is where this Step lives. Water is also associated with emotional healing, so get ready for the experience of the rebirth in the dark, wet womb. Of course, returning there is not possible, so we use the symbolic powers of a ritual bath to activate true healing.

Correspondences

Black is the witches' color, we all know that. But do you know why? It lets us protect ourselves both energetically and makes it easier to sneak around in the dark for all those secret things we do during the witching hours. Black is the color of the womb. All life springs from the dark. Are you already wearing a lot of black? That's your Inner Witch speaking. If not, embrace the dark shades in your wardrobe during this Step.

The number **one** is the number of beginnings. *Witch tip: Writing a number magically representing your focus on the inside of your left wrist gives you an added boost. Right now, I've got a big silver seven on mine. Each day when I set down to write, I trace over to charge it for the day.*

Botanicals

The two botanicals used in this step are **ginger** and **yarrow**, both in their dried form. Ginger is a root and we are using yarrow flowers. Other parts of yarrow can also be used, especially the branches and bark. Dried ground ginger is used because it is water soluble and combustible unlike fresh which has water rendering it neither of these things. Fresh ginger is much more potent (as is any fresh botanical) but must be worked with in a different manner. You can boil down fresh ginger into a refreshing tonic and magical water. I use the term "magical water" to refer to a base for making different potions (which are finished products used directly in spells). You'll be making a potion to use in the ritual bath out of these two botanicals.

Ginger

Properties: breaking curses (including emotional cords), courage, energy, healing, moon magic and release.

Associated energies: Lower Self, Under World, Root Chakra, South, Fire.

Yarrow

Properties: beginnings, challenges, emotions, fear, death, emotional strength, protection and witchcraft.

Associated energies: Lower Self, Under World, Upper World (death aspect), Higher Self (astrological magic, ceremonial workings).

Stone

Black obsidian, you can replace this with black onyx, jet or even hematite. Black obsidian is very different than other black stones, even ones with similar properties since it is technically a type of glass. A small smooth one is all that's needed for the technique in this Step.

Tarot

The Suit of Cups reflects emotions and water, so it is most appropriate for self-study and divination work during this lesson. You can place the Ace of Cups on your altar to activate your healing work. The Fool can be added to represent the new beginning brought through your healing work. The Magician, High Priestess and/or High Priest can be contemplated as a channel to unleashing your Inner Witch.

The Cup

The cup (chalice) is the first tool for your new altar. A black one is fantastic to represent healing. It's also great as a representation of releasing your Inner Witch. I recommend filling it with living water – from a body of water rather than the tap – placing it on your altar now. When you do this, ask the element of water to help you activate your emotions so you can really dive deep into the healing ahead.

Focus on Healing

If you read my blog, you'll know that I have done a lot of emotional healing to get to where I am today. I started teaching an earlier version of True Magic while I was still deep into my healing journey. When the signs all pointed to me to transforming the course into this book, I dove into the healing waters again. I tend to ignore my Lower Self, focusing too much on thoughts. Not surprising since I am a teacher and writer, but a balanced witch is a powerful one. Unleashing without temperance can lead to disastrous results, including a freaky boomerang effect of the shadow self. Don't worry, I've got your back. All the exercises in this book are proven effective.

Unleashing your Inner Witch is all about giving your true self permission to shine. It's all about the emotional depths of the Under World. Going into those dark corners and facing our fears. Only by staring them straight in the eyes can we tame them.

Witch, heal yourself and you can heal the world.

This step focuses on emotional healing using removal magic including grounding and cord cutting. You'll be making an incense and a potion. The technique of using stone spirit energy is practiced through creating a grounding charm with black obsidian. There are emotional cord cutting exercises. There is a Words of Power technique using the written word to remove your emotional connection to painful experiences and then transform them into beneficial feelings. This step culminates with a Releasing Ritual Bath where the final cord between your emotions and painful experiences is removed through immersion in salt water, one of the essential correspondences of the Under World and our Lower Selves.

The energy of the approach we're using is primarily Under World. Earlier, I talked about the Lower Self as the seat of our emotional energy. I also discussed how it is represented on the grand scale as Under World energy. You may be timid of the Under World. This is perfectly natural. Or you may be more comfortable in this realm. Either is fine. The Under World is represented by the dominion of the Sea. The energy is oceanic, so it's connected with the element of Water in this regard.

Witch's Hour of Power: Keep doing The True Magic Meditation daily.

Our Triple Nature

The image of the Triple Goddess is central to modern witchcraft, but we also have our own three-formed nature consisting of our thoughts, feelings and actions. These are our Three Functions.

Thoughts

The energy of thoughts is primarily more refined and thus situated in the Upper World. Our thoughts are the gateway to mystical experiences and are the core of our witchery. However, thoughts are deeply intertwined with emotions. The thoughts themselves don't cause a lot of trouble, it's the associated feelings that can lead us astray.

I want you to think of your thoughts as the verbal expressions of emotional energy. Emotions don't have words. It's the connection between the two that can give rise to destructive ways of thinking and being. The processes in this step are designed to remove the emotional attachment to your thoughts, particularly regarding painful experiences. Therefore, the practice of distress tolerance is introduced in this step. See your thoughts as the natural products of your emotions. They come and go. They don't control you, you are their master. That is the secret to a magical life and effective witchery.

Actions

Our behavior is another natural result of our emotions. The interconnections between our Three Functions are complex. Behavior that is self-destructive is the result of shadow energy, which is often caused by the harmful actions of others. Our addictions are the proof of the power of shadow energy transformed into actions. However, through the exercises in this step, you'll tame that shadow self. Whether the shadow is running our lives, or our true self is, this energy creates our reality. Truly in life, as in magic this is so.

"As within, so without.
As above, so below."

Feelings

Emotions fuel our thoughts and behaviors. Our emotions are our internal thermometer. Emotions are neither good nor bad. They simply ARE. All emotions have uses. What can happen when we are functioning from our shadow is that our range of emotions becomes truncated. We are left with anxiety, aggression, fear, hostility, frustration and their counterparts. Now all these feelings become destructive when they are the only ones we feel. They fuel the shadow which leads to higher levels of them being produced. So, it becomes a vicious circle. As humans we are wired to feel things. If we deprive ourselves of the range of emotions that we are capable of, the shadow emotions just continue to fill the void left by the other feelings. It sounds a bit complicated, but it's like eating junk food. Sticking with the fast food metaphor, how many of us have experienced that "Did I really just eat that?" moment after we've lost control? The feeling of loss of control is a key symptom that the shadow is running your life. When you feel in control of your life, you are operating from a place of alignment with the true self. The exercises in this step are designed to help you achieve just that.

A final note about the power of emotions: we have emotional memories for things we have experienced, but this also gets instantly applied to new situations. We tap into what we already know to interpret this experience and just by firing up neural connections; emotions that are associated with the bits of the new experience we recognize are activated. This is tricky business! Practicing techniques like grounding and cord cutting help to sever the emotions from the original memory making us less likely to have the association spread to new experience. It's like getting rid of a weed at the root rather than just picking the flower above the surface. This is deep work, going into those roots. Be gentle with yourself.

Acceptance

It's easy to write "be gentle with yourself," but much more challenging to practice. Acceptance is the way to finding self-compassion. You may wonder why I put acceptance here in the very first step. It's because we must accept what has happened before we can sever the emotional tether to it. Regarding witchcraft, this is the absolute first step in any working. We need to put our energy into solving a problem rather than resisting its existence. When we do this, we clear the path for developing intentions that will lead to the outcomes we desire. Resistance is like spiritual or energetic dirt. We need to be purified from it through acceptance.

Radically accepting the past is an incredibly healing experience. It's also liberating when we cut the emotional cord with those memories. I like to think that the cord between emotions and painful memories is the fuel line to the shadow self. Cut it and the shadow's tank is quickly emptied.

Never confuse acceptance with approval. You aren't saying that what was done to you is okay, it's not. You are acknowledging that it happened.

Distress Tolerance

Acceptance requires acknowledging not only what has happened in the past (and your current state of affairs) but also accepting the emotions that accompany the memories. The memories themselves don't have any way of harming you. It's anger, anxiety, bitterness, despair, distress, fear, grief, sadness and rage that are the problem. And the issue isn't the emotions themselves, it's the cord between them and your past. That's why we use the cord cutting technique. The process is simple, but the process complex.

Feel. Deal. Heal.

Part of the acceptance process is to learn to tolerate distressing emotions such as the ones I've mentioned above. When we can experience the emotions without resistance, we feel them and can release them. Fighting the feelings strengthens the dysfunctional cord. Emotions naturally come up during the day. Someone does something nice for us and we are grateful. You have an easy morning commute to work and you are happy. You're grumpy for no obvious reason.

I think it's on social media that our collective intolerance of emotional distress is most evident. Everyone is butt-hurt about minor insults and differences of opinions. Yes, it makes us angry when someone disagrees, or slings hate. Accept that. But don't let the feeling decide your thoughts or actions. Accept the situation. Let the distressing emotions have their say. Release them through techniques like journaling, cord cutting and grounding. Use correspondences to assist you. This is sinking into realness, which we do with the ritual bath ritual at the end of the step. We are washed clean through accepting what was and what is. We accept that only we can shape how we use these experiences – either to become stuck or to grow. In realness there is growth. In falsity, there is only the shadow. That's the magic of acceptance.

Witches accept all emotions for we are confident in our power to control our reactions to them.

Emotional Magic

So those are the psychological aspects of acceptance and distress tolerance, which have magical powers in and of themselves, but here's where mastering these skills really translates to witchery. True magic is energetic. Emotions live entirely in the world of force. Exploring them, sitting with them, learning to master them through realness hones the same skills necessary for working with mystical forces, like the realms. Our spells often seek to alter our feelings. We want to mend our broken heart or alleviate loneliness in love spells, for example. In prosperity magic, we want to manifest contentment and remove stress associated with finances. I think we get so caught up in writing a great intention, picking out the best correspondences and developing power incantations that we forget that the root of magic is emotional. A lot of magic is about alleviating distress. The better we understand the distressing emotions, the more capable we are of manifesting relief from the situation that has caused us upset. The work you do in this step helps you to understand your emotions better, so you'll be able to summon energy better. If you don't want to be sad it's best if you fully acknowledge what it feels like rather than to push against it. Leaning into these feelings rather than backing away is True Magic.

Sink into realness. That's where the True Magic lives.

Emotional magic like cord cutting activates painful memories and powerful feelings. Techniques like casting a protective circle, transmutation or supportive correspondences to help us remove excess emotional energy.

Witch's Hour of Power: Journaling

The written word has so much power. If you are new to writing about your experiences, and this seems daunting to you, I recommend starting by setting a timer for five minutes.

Write about the most mundane details – what you wore, ate, the weather, etc. – if you aren't comfortable with writing about your feelings, plans, etc. Whatever you write about, do it for a set period of time that's achievable. Do it every day for a few weeks. This will become a habit. Before you know it, you'll miss it when you don't write. Avoid getting trapped in thinking that you must write some profound. Just write.

Writing is creating. Creativity is the source of True Magic.

Separate journal entries on the concepts introduced in each step is a fantastic practice. So far, we've covered acceptance, resistance, emotional distress, realness, shadow, true self and emotional magic. Write whatever comes to mind. Don't research the topics. Just write what you think. Then do all the research you like. Witches love knowledge. Those are seven topics to take you through a week's worth of five minutes of writing/day. That will get your creative juices flowing.

Making Incense and Potion

While you're working on the journaling exercise, you can get busy creating the healing herbal blend. You'll need a mortar and pestle to mix the yarrow and ginger. A kettle or pot to boil the water for the potion is also required, even better is a tea pot with a built-in strainer. A glass jar with lid for storage the healing blend is a good idea.

Instructions

Set up the kitchen with a protective black candle. Spread out your black work cloth and then place the ingredients, tools and supplies on it. You can also make black labels for the Healing Potion and the Healing Incense, either using black ink or white ink on black paper. Another tip to fully activate the energy of the incense and potion is to wrap them jar and bottle in clean, black cloth. I usually make a little "hat" out of the fabric that I tie using corresponding colors to the top of a jar or bottle. Every little bit helps.

Preparing the Botanicals for Use

I recommend removing any herbs or plants being used for magic from their original packaging. Most things are best kept in sealed glass jars out of direct exposure to light. Specific plants may vary in their needs. Our ground ginger and dried yarrow flowers are happiest in jars in your witch's cupboard, away from light.

If you want to harness specific attributes of any botanical, whether in a blend or on their own, you can perform a simple ritual to bind them for your purpose. For preparing ginger and yarrow for use in the potion, incense and tonic, you want to attune them to their properties appropriate for emotional removal magic. Choose the ones that make sense from the list above.

Connect with the plant spirit. Holding the botanical in your hand, envision the plant from which it came. Ask the plant spirit "What is there for me to know about you?" Listen to any messages. Specific info should be recorded in your BoS (Book of Shadows).

Next state your intention. For example, you are using the ginger for purification and the yarrow for protection. Explain this to the plant spirit, asking for their assistance for your magical intentions. Thank the plant for lending its energies.

When you are doing this simple technique with a plant spirit, you may find that you are being pulled to a deeper connection to it. I have several plant spirits that I have a relationship with, from my close spiritual connection with Rose to my household love for Sage. I posted a link in the Further Reading section at the end of the step if you are interested in learning more about Plant Spirits.

Use this technique with all botanicals and ingredients used in any working.

Making Incense

To combine botanicals into an incense, you want to use a method that is aligned to the energies that you'll be utilizing in the plants. Since they are being used for removal magic in this step, you'll want to macerate them enough to release their compounds using counter clockwise circles with the pestle. Seven good turns should do nicely with these two since they are very amenable botanicals. More challenging ones like most of the poisons require a more intricate preparation process. Once ready, store the herbs in a sealed glass jar. If you have an extra piece of obsidian on hand (in addition to the one in the grounding exercise further on in this step) you can cleanse it in a salt bag or under the full moon and then slip it in with the incense. The shared properties will mingle together quite nicely.

Using the Incense

To burn the incense: Right now, the incense contains ALL the different energies of the ginger and yarrow. If you are going to burn them in a general way, you can put a little nest under the charcoal, light it and then put more on top. The ginger might crackle a bit. The smell will be very earthy, conjuring up that Under World energy of this step.

Making and Using the Potion

For the potion, boil two cups of spring, distilled or salt water. Add 1 tsp. ground ginger and 1 tbsp. dried yarrow flowers. Cover. Let sit until cooled. Store in sealed glass bottle in cupboard. This is enough for the ritual bath and to fill your altar chalice. Since the aromatic smell of this potion is very earthy, you can add another Under World essence to it for a more appealing bath smell, such as rose water.

Making and Using the Daily Tonic

For drinking as a daily tonic: add a pinch of ginger and 1 tsp. yarrow to tea infuser or directly in mug of boiled water. General health tonic – will aid in emotional healing, improve digestion, sleep, etc. If you have any health conditions or take medications, use responsibly.

Grounding

Grounding is a technique for connecting ourselves to the present moment. If you're feeling disconnected from your surroundings or your own internal states, too involved with others' problems, buzzing from energy in the natural environment or generally stressed out, grounding yourself is quite helpful. Grounding can also release excess emotions. We also need to ground ourselves before and after doing magic. Prior to magic, getting grounded helps us to remove any of the things mentioned earlier. Afterwards, it returns us to the Middle World, so we can get on with our everyday lives.

Basic Technique

The basic imagery for grounding is found in the True Magic Meditation: envision deep black roots running through your body, collecting all that doesn't serve you well and then see those roots connecting to the earth, extending deep down. Mentality "sweep" the excess of whatever it is into those roots. Release into the earth, knowing it will be recycled anew. Pull your roots up when finished.

Grounding Using Physical Cues

The simplest form of grounding consists of focusing on different parts of the physical environment. Whenever you are feeling overwhelmed or disconnected from reality (whether after a working or in everyday life), pull yourself back to your body by asking and answering these questions:

- What is one thing I can see?
- What is one thing I can smell?
- What is one thing I can feel?
- What is one thing I can hear?

Develop a detailed description in your mind's eye for each question, as though you were doing so for a friend on the phone.

Grounding only takes a few moments and can be added to your Witch's Hour of Power as part of your daily practice.

Next Level Grounding

Sometimes you may need a more intense grounding technique if you're really soaring high after a metaphysical experience or dealing with a lot of stress or horrible people. It's helpful to take several deep breaths then envision yourself as a tree. Your feet connect to the earth beneath you, releasing all the excess emotional energy down into the ground where it will be reborn anew. Envision that your thought overload is releasing up to the heavens where it will also be recycled into something of value. As you release these unnecessary feelings and thoughts, envision pulling in calming energy from both sources.

Stone Spirit Magic and Charm

Black obsidian has several properties that are well suited for our emotional healing using removal magic: death, emotions, emotional transformation, grounding, magic, personal growth and protection. Black obsidian is also associated with the #1 making it an ideal choice for the first step. The charm is made now to offer protection as you continue onto the more intense Words of Power exercise.

Preparation

Getting any object ready for magical use requires two steps: purification and activation. Cleansing can be easily accomplished by placing the black obsidian in a salt bag for a few days. You want to remove any gunk on it as well as nonessential properties. You'll know the obsidian is ready when it feels noticeably lighter than it did before. Note that you may need to frequently cleanse the obsidian during this step as it will accumulate the emotional "dirt" you're releasing through the cord cutting activities. Activation occurs when an object has specific properties released while others are subdued. This can be accomplished by "smoking" the herbs by passing them through the smoke from the incense you made. Although the overall energy is of removal magic, in this step you are performing attraction magic because you want to bind the properties of the incense to the stone, attracting like to like to activate the obsidian. So, pass the stone through the smoke in a clockwise (attracting) motion. Seven passes should do it. If the stone still feels heavy, do it a bit more.

Stone Spirit Connection

Now that the obsidian is attuned to the intended purpose, it's time to connect with it to infuse your intention into it. Once this occurs, it has become a charm (or amulet if you prefer). I usually use the term "charm" to indicate a magical object consisting of a single item. I use "amulet" to denote multiple objects. This means they are fused into one magical creation. You can then practice transferring energy into it to achieve a grounded state.

Creating a Protected Magical Space

I recommend doing your daily meditation immediately prior to creating this circle. You should also wash up.

- Choose a location where you won't be disturbed for the duration of the exercise.
- Wear comfortable clothing.
- Tidy the space and make sure you wash up before beginning the activity.

- Once you are comfortably seated, without your energy centers crossed (i.e., arms and legs don't overlap), begin to create the space.
- Taking your right arm, draw a magic circle in front of you. Envision this circle expands to include your space (i.e., any props or tools are included). See the circle become a sphere that extends above your head and below your feet. Do this three times.

When your working is complete, in this case the charm activation, you need to release the space.

Creating the Charm

Like what you did with the botanicals, envision a cord between you and the obsidian. Greet the stone. Let its color and energy travel across the cord to you. State your intention of asking the stone to become a receptacle for your excess emotions and energy to help you become grounded. Contemplate the emptiness of the stone. It is waiting to receive that which no longer serves you. In the protected space, release any excess emotions down through the cord. Experience the feeling of release. On the in-breath, pull the cord to your emotional seat in your root energy center (chakra). On the out-breath release all the excess down through it into the stone. Repeat several times. When finished, thank the stone for their service. If the stone is already heavier, cleanse it again in the salt. Once it is purified again, activate it with the incense and carry it with you so that you can do an energetic "dump and run" anytime you need to ground.

Opening the Magic Circle

Now that you've finished the activation of the charm, open the circle. Envision the protective circle shrinking to include only you and your charm. Journal about the experience and record the technique in your BoS. If you aren't familiar with creating magic space this way, you can practice it until you feel comfortable.

Removal and Reversal Magic

Once your obsidian is ready for use again, you are ready to do the ritual below. You'll need black paper and a white marker (paint pens work great) or white paper with black marker. Use a piece of white or black string to represent the cord between your emotions and the memory along with scissors to cut the cord. You'll also use the incense again in the working and use the circle technique from the charm creation exercise.

There are two techniques used in this working: removal and reversal magic. You've done removal magic in the grounding charm exercise. It is simply a working that takes something away, like excess energy, a toxic person, or obstacles. Removal magic is best done during the waning moon. Protection magic is a type of removal work since it removes existing negative energies and potential ones. Reversal magic goes one step further by taking that which we removed and reversing its properties to our benefit. The type of reversal magic you'll be doing is known as transmutation.

Witch's Words of Power Ritual

This exercise brings emotional healing by releasing the connection of our emotions to a painful memory. Begin by organizing your space with paper and markers, a fresh black (or white) candle, the incense and your grounding stone. Follow the steps from that exercise to create your magic space. Once created, light the candle (which you'll throw out after this working) and the incense. Keep the stone nearby. If you start to feel overwhelmed during the ritual, do the release technique to ground yourself.

Envision yourself completely surrounded by a protective circle. Nothing can harm you here, not even the memory you are about to evoke. When you are ready, record the memory on one of the blank sheets. Ground as you need to.

Next, write a list of the emotions you feel now that the memory has been activated on a separate sheet. Roll up each sheet. Tie the string to each roll. Continue to ground as necessary into your charm. You may be feeling intense emotions at this point. You are safe in the circle; the charm is supporting you and the exercise ends with a reversal of these emotions.

Hold the cord over the candle, using scissors to cut the cord. You can also sever the cord in the flame of the candle if you are comfortable doing that. Take the memory sheet and destroy it by burning or putting it in the trash (and getting it out of your house as soon as possible.) The memory exists but no longer has emotions connected to it. You can safely revisit the memory when necessary, but you don't want its energy lurking about.

Now turn your attention to the list of emotions. How do you feel reading the list? Thank each one, then cross it off and write beside it a beneficial one. For example, replace "anger" with "compassion" and "sadness" with "joy." This is the reversal part of the ritual. Now take time to feel each of the beneficial emotions. You should be feeling much more grounded now. When you are ready, open the circle. Record the technique in your BoS. You can apply removal and reversal magic to a great many problems using this cord cutting technique.

Emotional Healing Through the Power of a Ritual Bath

You've already engaged in purification practices – cleansing objects and tools, the importance of washing up before rituals and purifying space using a magic circle. Purification has been part of mystical practices throughout history. Through cleansing, we remove "dirt – real and energetic – from ourselves and the objects involved in our witchery. The last exercise for this step is on purification through ritual bathing. In our ritual, the emphasis is on removing the last vestiges of shadow energy. However, the ritual bath should be done for the purpose of cleansing and preparation before major workings, such as casting a spell. Through the watery Under World symbolism of immersing ourselves in water, we enter the energetic depths, releasing all that harms us into the waters. Conveniently, when we pull the plug that water goes into the Under World of the pipes.

Supplies:

- Epsom or Sea Salts (unscented). You can add a scoop of activated charcoal if you like. Activated charcoal is purified to a higher degree than the briquettes used for burning incense. Salt is a powerful protector and absorber while charcoal is a mighty purifier.
- Healing Potion. You can add a few drops of an essence, oil or water of an associated Under World botanical that has a pleasant smell if you want to the potion you made. Examples: honeysuckle, rose water, jasmine.
- Fresh white candle to symbolize your rebirth since this is the last part of your emotional healing journey. The white candle is your spirit borne anew.
- Burn the incense if possible.
- Shamanic drum music if possible. My favorite is anything by Byron Metcalfe.
- Something from the sea, like a shell or stone to represent the Under World energy of the ocean.

Procedure:

- Timing: On the last night of the waning moon. That way you can begin your new life on the first day of the new cycle. The dark moon (the astrological new moon) is the liminal "buffer zone" between the old and the new. Take this time to reflect on this step and all your work.
- Bring all your supplies into the bathroom. Cast your circle first and then run the water. Add the salt (and charcoal if using) first, sending your intention to be purified of

the past and born anew into it as you stir it in the water. Then add the potion – all two cups except for enough for your altar chalice. While you stir, contemplate the healing power of the Under World oceanic current. Once the ingredients are in the tub, get in and chant the incantation as many times as you need to:

- *"Mighty sea, release from me, all that binds and troubles my mind, into the deeps below does the connection between my feelings and the past go."*
- While the music is playing, concentrate on releasing all those destructive emotions into the water. Release the cord to them as a gift which they will readily accept. Messages and images often come forward during this post-release moment while you are still in trance.
- When you feel ready, light the white candle: *"Born from the depths this night, my past has taken flight. Now this candle I do light and look to the future bright."*
- Drain the water and open the circle.
- Write about the experience in your journal.

Elemental Healing Ritual

I'm including this ritual as an added boost to the rest of the work in this step. You can do it now and whenever you're in need of healing.

Supplies

Five white candles
Picture of yourself that reflects happiness and wholeness
Dirt, steam, water, smoke (i.e., from burning incense)

Prepare candles by removing nonessential energy using the method of your choice. Dressing with an oil suitable, almond and olive are two examples. For this ritual dress them in a counter clockwise manner. Once dressed, it's always helpful to rub the candles or sprinkle with the botanicals being used in the spell.

* If you can't burn candles or incense, battery operated ones will do nicely. Consider using an electric scent diffuser.

Choosing an incense to burn for any ritual is always based on the practitioner(s) and the magic at hand. I'll suggest yarrow burnt on charcoal or oak essential oil or essence (alcohol based). This is a gentle healing ritual so it's best to avoid super intense botanicals (e.g., mugwort, sage, lavender), the resins (i.e., frankincense) or strong essential oils. You want healing that is powerful and extended rather than a one-off boost.

Preparation

Ritual cleansing of the body, mind and space is imperative for healing rituals. I always say that but who am I kidding? At least wash your hands first. I usually do that much. Salt is excellent for removal and purification, consider adding activated charcoal (which is not the same as regular) to your bath. Black obsidian can also be added to the bath. I've got a black obsidian healing ritual available in The Witches' Realm.

Your ritual space should be cleansed beforehand, removing unnecessary clutter.

Arrange the elemental symbols according to the cardinal points: earth – north, air – east, fire – south, water – west. Place one candle on the inside of each. Place your photo at the top with a candle in front.

Steam: pour boiling water into a heat-proof bowl or mug then cover.

Smoke: burning incense*

Dirt: bowl of earth (preferably fresh from a healthy wooded area)

Water: living water (from the sea or a freshwater source, bottled spring can be substituted).

* If the smoke isn't possible for you, substitute with a flame (even from a lighter or a picture).

The Ritual

To the elements surrounding me, I release my pain.

Hold bowl with earth at your heart center. Concentrate on feeling the dark coolness. Once connected, release your pain out through your breath into the earth. Do this three times, then say:

To the north, the land of the earth, bury my pain.

Place bowl back in original spot.

Remove the lid from your steam bowl. Raise to heart center. Concentrate on the moist air rising up. Once connected, release your pain out through your breath into the air. Do this three times, then say:

To the east, the land of air, blow away my pain.

Replace the air bowl. Light the incense, hold the fire bowl at heart center (be sure your hair, etc. is out of the way). Concentrate on the rising smoke. Once connected, release your pain out through your breath into the smoke. Do this three times, then say:

To the south, the land of fire, burn my pain.

Replace the fire bowl. Pick up the water bowl, hold at heart center. Concentrate on the liquid. Once connected, release your pain out through your breath into the water. Do this three times, then say:

To the west, the land of water, drown my pain.

Pause here to continue to release into the elements. When ready, begin the healing section of the ritual.

From the elements around me, I accept healing.

Light the candle beside the earth bowl.

From the north, I accept the healing of the earth.

Feel the healing energy of the earth rise from deep beneath you, entering through the soles of your feet and spreading through your body.

Light the candle beside the air bowl.

From the east, I accept the healing of wind.

Feel the healing energy of the air come down from above until it encircles you.

Light the candle beside the fire bowl.

From the south, I accept the healing of fire.

Feel the flame spread from your heart center through your entire body.

Light the candle beside the water bowl.

From the west, I accept the healing of water.

Feel the soothing healing of water running through your veins.

Light the candle beside your picture.

I am committed to healing my emotions, thoughts and body.

Concentrate on connecting to the picture of your happy, authentic self (aka the fifth element, spirit). Recall how you felt in that moment, letting the energy flood your body, mingling with the elemental healing forces. When ready, release the elements by extinguishing the candles: *element of earth, I release you from this space* and so on. Leave your candle by the picture for a while after, envisioning your healthiest, most authentic self. When ready, end the ritual:

> *Out of perfect trust and perfect love, I have released my pain*
> *And I am healing.*
> *As within, so without*
> *As above, so below.*
> *It is so!*

Open the circle however you usually do.

Dispose of the soiled elemental symbols. You can continue with the candle lighting healing part of the ritual daily. Process any images or messages that came through during the ritual.

Completing This Step

Keep your chalice on your altar. You can add a black candle, or one marked with black, feeling the power of your unleashed Inner Witch activate. Feel the remarkable energy of not being chained. Ground any excess energy.

Remember to continue with your Witch's Hour of Power practices, including the meditation, grounding and carrying your obsidian charm.

Further Reading

I often write about healing on my Keeping Her Keys Patheos blog. Here is a selection of my articles:

Elemental Healing Ritual: http://www.patheos.com/blogs/ keepingherkeys/2018/06/elemental-healing-ritual/
Healing the Mother Wound: http://www.patheos.com/blogs/ keepingherkeys/2018/05/the-witch-and-the-mother-wound/

Let It Go Energy Grid: http://www.patheos.com/blogs/keep
ingherkeys/2018/07/waning-moon-magick-let-that-st-go-
energy-grid/
Healing from Trauma with the Three Keys Ritual: http://www.
patheos.com/blogs/keepingherkeys/2017/12/hekate-and-
healing-from-trauma/
Three Simple Spells Using the Tarot and Herbs: http://www.
patheos.com/blogs/keepingherkeys/2018/05/three-simple-
removal-personal-development-spells/

Books
Paul Beryl, *Master Book of Herbalism*
More on working with the elements: Sorita D'Este and David
Rankine, *Practical Elemental Magic*
* Sandra Kynes, *Llewellyn's Complete Book of Correspondences*
Sandra Kynes, 365 Days of Crystal Magic: Simple Practices with
Gemstones and Minerals

Blog
Courtney Weber, A Guide to Forgiveness (By a Witch Who
Sucks at Forgiving): http://www.patheos.com/blogs/double
toilandresist/2018/08/a-guide-to-forgiveness-by-a-witch-
who-sucks-at-forgiving/
Scarlet Magdalene, Importance of Self Care During Intense Magic:
http://www.patheos.com/blogs/teaaddictedwitch/2018/04/
self-care-in-intense-magical-practice/

Relationships

I don't need fame or fortune,
what I need is a few people who are with me. Beside me. Walking a
similar path. Who listen when I speak. And pay attention when I don't.
Those people who make it all worth it. Who make my heart smile and
my mind happy. Who teach me what love is. Show me how to do life
right.
Who have risen to the heights. Who are born of fire. That ooze
authenticity. That walk with their shadow. Who get my weirdness
because they either share it or have their own.
Give me a handful of those people.
They're all I need to get by.

Starting This Step

Relationships are our blessing and bane. We all need at least one
person who truly gets us. Even our relationship with that person
can be strained at times. I find relationships so fascinating
because they are purely an energetic thing. So much magic in
them, for sure. The journey out of the emotional realm of the
Under World continues with an exploration on the energy of
others through practice, understanding, technique, ritual and
learning about ourselves and the energetic objects that can
augment our relationships.

The Dark Moon

The Dark Moon (astrological New Moon, check the lunar phase
tables for your local date and time) is the night for the major
working of this Step. The energy of the Dark Moon is the same
in intensity as the Full Moon, but the nature of the current is the
opposite. The Dark Moon represents the end of a cycle, drawing
unto itself all that needs to be left in the past. The ritual focus in
this step is on cleansing relationship cords. This can either be for

a specific relationship or for cleansing your cords with others in a general way. The intent is to remove "dirt" that accumulates through misunderstandings, communication problems and other normal hassles. This is a great technique for relationships that you're stuck with – from your ex with whom you share a child to your annoying boss.

The Under World and the Element of Air

This Step is all about combining emotions with the airy quality of thoughts and words. Our relationships with others and our general way of orienting ourselves towards humans is often primarily driven by our emotions. We're not out of the Under World yet! Air is very much the essence of communication, which comprises a lot of the practices contained in this step. We spend a lot of time working with boundaries in this Step. They also serve to help develop your focus and self-discipline, two very important abilities for effective witchery.

Correspondences

To symbolize this "light at the end of the tunnel," the color for this step is **yellow** which is also symbolic of the element of air. **Two** is the number of combing which is what you'll be doing throughout this step.

Botanicals

Our botanicals include **sage** and a wood suitable for a wand, like **ash, poplar or rowan**. Sage is fantastic for protection, cleansing the body, soul and space. It's also highly useful for "opening the way" in any working. Other abilities of sage include clarity, fertility, love, protection and well-being. Sage can be burned on its own or as part of an incense. It's safe to consume in small amounts unless contraindicated by a health condition, if it wasn't processed using harmful chemicals. Growing sage in the home offers continual protection and supports healthy relationships (and good cheer).

If you're already well versed in the wonders of sage, I encourage you to explore these two lesser known herbals that are great for relationship magic:

- Betony: calming; protection; reversal magic
- Skullcap: binding; especially for relationship attachments

Note that these are quite potent, so use with caution.

The tree worked with in this step is three variations of related ones: ash, poplar or rowan. All three are strongly associated with protection and witchcraft. They can be burnt in fires or added to an incense. You can make a magical water using the potion technique from Step 1. The way they are used in this Step is as a wand, probably their most common magical application.

Stone

Associated with all these correspondences is the stone for the step, yellow **citrine**. It brings balance, connection and protection. Good for all partnerships (including romantic ones), this stone is used in a protection amulet that helps us connect to others in a healthy way. You can also work with rose quartz for love, protection, heart healing and connection.

Tarot

For the Tarot enthusiasts, the Suit of Swords, The Lovers, The Magician (#1) and the High Priestess (#2) are great for contemplating during this Step. Ideas for using the cards in this way can be found at the back of this book.

Witches' Hour of Power: Add a daily Tarot card reading.
While concentrating on the day ahead, shuffle the cards or focus on the app until the right moment comes to pull one. Keep a record of them in your journal.

The Wand

Wands are a bridge between our internal power supply and the external forces. Some witches prefer one special one and others, like me, have different ones for various uses. Wands can be associated with specific elements or more general use. If you don't already have a favored one, magical questing for one can be so much fun.

Wand Quest

Sometimes objects spontaneously appear without us even having to intentionally seek them. The best personal story I have of this is the time that I was out for a run in an urban neighborhood when I practically tripped over a fist-sized chunk of black obsidian in the middle of the sidewalk. You've developed your observation skills to the point now that correspondences that you need to be working with may be spontaneously presenting themselves to you in a similar manner.

However, we can also go on a journey to find the right ones. This quest can be a metaphysical journey, an actual adventure or both. Get out and explore your world for that perfect piece of wood for your wand. Connecting to the energies of nature is an excellent way to let your Inner Witch out.

Planning Your Correspondence Quest

Write an intention on a piece of paper that you can bring with you on your quest.

Location

The more remote, the better the location is for receiving an object such as your wand. Although it's possible to have a correspondence come forward to you in a more urban environment, there's a lot of nonessential and unnatural energies swirling about.

Revisit special places. I used to go to this large urban park a few times a week. I used to wander down the less traveled trails, searching for cool places for rituals. One day I found such a place. It even had a bench and a dining-room table sized rock. If you don't have a spot like this, maybe your first quest is to find it!

Research the parks and nature reserves in your area if you don't have a location already selected. Get outside! The best witchery is always done in nature.

The Quest Begins

- Copy your intention from your Book of Shadows onto a piece of paper that you can carry with you. Don't forget a backpack and plastic bags to carry home your wand and other correspondence(s).
- When you arrive at the location, read the intention out loud.
- Pay attention to your surroundings. Notice the plants, any wildlife and the built environment. A witch is an observer of all things because we know that signs are there waiting for us to discover them.
- The wand will present itself to you once you are open to receive it. It may be in an odd place. If you're looking for other objects they will be something unusual, such as the hunk of black obsidian I found or an unexpected animal sighting. I've had so many of these! Land-locked ducks in the middle of a blizzard, snakes in my urban driveway and in the pool, a lone feather on the shore. If it's an animal sighting, then you won't have anything to carry home with you except the creature's energy.
- When you find your wand or other object, ask it if it is yours. The energy from it will be your answer.
- The wand or other object will not be harmful to remove from a site.

After the Quest

- Cleanse the wand or other object only if it feels necessary.
- Sit with your new wand. Hold it in your hands, study it. Get to know each other.
- Research the standard applications of your wand but use it how it feels right to you.
- Record the information about the wand in your Book of Shadows, including the lunar phase and planetary considerations. You may want to develop your own correspondence database with this information in it.
- Continue to build your relationship with the wand in the way that feels right to you. You can keep it on your altar, sleep with it beside you or carry it next to your skin.
- Embellish your wand with its own correspondences, including symbols, colors, bones, feathers, stones, ribbons and other items.
- Once it's prepared, hold a simple dedication ceremony for the wand, asking it to work well for you. You can bless it with sage smoke.

Metaphysical Correspondence Quest

If it's not possible to go on an actual adventure, you can have your correspondence(s) revealed to you in the Other World using various techniques such as a journey, fire scrying or ask your ancestor to send you in the right direction.

Healthy Relationships

It does take two, at least most of the time. The basic way that we view ourselves is as individuals and in connection to others. We tackle sovereignty in the next step before that let's clear the way by working on some of the ways that the energy of others impacts our lives and witchery.

The witches' world is full of others. Nowhere is this more evident than in our circle casting, where we either draw others in or keep them out. Relationships exist in the world of force. The energy of two individuals combines to create a third – the relationship – that exists purely in the world of force but takes form in the everyday world. Emotions are at the heart of most relationships. Many of our closest ones provide us with a sense of completeness. A feeling of closing the circle on our identity.

I believe that witches are drawn to others because of we are often energy junkies. We innately crave the delicious feelings of belonging, and as curious creatures love to study others. Some of us may need to be with others constantly while there are those who love their solitude. Our personality characteristics and experiences largely shape how we approach all interpersonal relationships. Knowing ourselves can really help us deal with toxic people.

Tips for Dealing with Toxic People

- Know your own boundaries. See my lists of healthy and unhealthy ones at the end of this post. Explore them and reinforce them daily.
- Be compassionate and empathetic. If this is a struggle for you, see the previous tip. Being kind to toxic people doesn't mean putting up with their harmful ways, but it does require us to consider whether they are just having a bad day, are hungry or maybe aren't great with words. Pausing to reflect before categorizing someone as toxic is a sure sign that you aren't.
- Be forgiving...to a point. My general rule is: treat me badly once, shame on you. Twice? That's on me. If you let someone treat you poorly, they aren't going to stop no matter how much you care. Again, refer to my point about boundaries.
- If someone is harming you, insulting you or "love bombing" you (excessive praise and gifts), enforce those boundaries. Walk away. Hit the block button. Self-compassion comes

first.

- We all can get trapped in toxicity. That's because we have all been wounded and have shadow selves. The Witches' Journey is about healing these aspects and growth. Stagnation is a sure sign of toxicity.
- A touch of humor is often helpful in dealing with toxic people. However, they can be very damaging. I've included some healing and dealing resources at the end of this article.

Boundaries

Boundaries are the energetic barriers we put between ourselves and others. They are our own person circle that we cast. Understanding your personal boundaries and the consequence for when they are violated is an important skill to develop as a witch. Since you are engaged in energy work, may be an empath or a psychic, and probably are a healer of some sort, it's important to have firm barriers so that you don't get sucked into another's harmful energy. After you study the tables, I encourage you to contemplate your own in the exercise below.

Healthy Boundaries
Signs of Healthy Boundaries
Appropriate trust
Asking a person before touching them
Moving slowly towards intimacy
Not seeking validation from another
Being focused on your own development
Trusting your decisions
Self-respect
Respecting others
Valuing differing opinions
Not tolerating unacceptable actions or words
Being compassionate to yourself

Being compassionate to others

Gradual self-disclosure

Being wary of others who come on too strong, too fast (i.e., love bombing)

Defining your own truth (magical life)

Appreciating others' truths

Saying "yes" to things that genuinely appeal to you

Saying "no" to unwanted attention of all kinds

Clearly communicating your needs and wants

Understanding that others may have difficulty communicating

Noticing and acting when someone crosses your boundaries

Observing others' boundaries and noting inappropriate behavior and actions.

Unhealthy Boundaries

Signs of Unhealthy Boundaries

Trusting or distrusting without reason

Touching people without asking

Jumping quickly into a relationship or situation without mindful contemplation

Defining yourself by how you want others to see and treat you

Being overly involved in others' lives

Not listening to your own inner voice

Creating drama for attention

Disrespecting others

Having a rigid mindset

Tolerating others behavior that you find unacceptable to avoid rejection

Losing yourself in a relationship

Judging people harshly without cause

Revealing everything about yourself to people who don't know well

Getting caught up by someone's charm
Letting other people define your life
Ignoring others' opinions
Saying "yes" to things that violate your boundaries
Being involved in hurtful talk or actions involving others
Expecting people to read your mind
Not seeing the world from others perspective
Being unaware of your own boundaries and their consequences
Abuse and addiction of all kinds

Knowing Your Limits

Explore the times when someone has crossed the line with you. What was it that caused them to violate your limits? Make a list of absolute lines that others can't cross without consequences. Take these boundary definitions and turn them into affirmations. For example, if hate speech is a boundary for you can write a statement like "I will protect those who are marginalized." This moves the energy of the boundary from being dependent on the actions of others to your own sovereign principles. It's a form of reversal magic.

Protection Magic

Creating your own protection amulet involves choosing the appropriate intention and then matching appropriate correspondences to create a powerful object. I generally refer to an amulet as having a minimum of three ingredients, while a charm has one two. Regardless of an amulet or charm, starting with a stone or crystal that represents the spirit of our intention forms a solid foundation for the object. Often, a charm or amulet is created by infusing our intention into it, using a technique like the one used in the first step. Then we can further enhance the object by adding a symbol or developing a special sigil. In the next step, we'll get into developing a personal one.

Citrine Amulet for Happy Relationships

I used yellow citrine (previously cleansed), our stone for this step, as the base. I surrounded the stone with gold metallic polymer clay, shaping a hole so I could put a cord through it once it was completed. After I baked it and let it cool, I wrote the infinity symbol on it – first in white then overlaid in gold. While drawing the symbol, I envisioned the cord that connects me to my loved ones as well as the wider one between me and all others. I smoked it using sage to activate the amulet. A finishing touch was to put it on a key ring with one of my personal symbols, the elephant. Now I can carry it with me where ever I go.

Honoring Ancestors

I mentioned the large cord, really a million of them that connect us with all others. As witches, we can tug on those cords with our rituals. I am limiting the scope of this Step to our connection with other humans, but we often have close relationships with all manner of entities, from deities to stones. Our human relationships can exist in the Middle World or purely in the realms. One example is in working with ancestors, those formerly living humans that have passed from this life. You may not always see them, but your ancestors are always with you.

Each life lived creates an energetic location in the cosmic consciousness that can be accessed by others and can also take form as a spirit in the Middle World. Our ancestors can include biological family members, nonbiological family such as friends and soul mates and others whom were important to us when they were in this life. In addition, our witchy ancestors may come forward to us or we may seek their "location" in the cosmos. Doreen Valiente is an ancestor that I honor through acts and a small shrine. You may also become connected to an ancestor whose work greatly resonates with you, such as a political leader, activist, writer, musician or artist.

Incorporating Ancestors into your Practice

There are many ways to incorporate ancestors in your practice, including:

- Creating an ancestor shrine with pictures, objects and other representations. You can leave offerings at appropriate times using favored food and drink.
- Having a quiet supper where the ancestors' favorite dishes are served, a place is set for them and the tone is kept quiet. I've given up on the idea of a silent supper because none of us can make it through, but we do tone it down. This can be held on the ancestors' birthday, other special day or around the first of November.
- Seeking their assistance in magic. You can petition an ancestor for support and intervention.
- Using representations of them in spells. This is a technique I've used quite a bit. Ask the ancestor for their assistance and then activate their energy by including a belonging of theirs or a representation (like a picture of Queen Doreen) directly in your spell, such as a Witch's Jar or amulet.
- Conduct a ritual honoring your ancestors. You can include the ones I've mentioned before, but also the ancestors of the place where you live.

The True Magic Circle

The witches' circle is an energetic boundary where we can exclude all others save for the forces at hand, we cast the circle not only to raise the cone of power but to keep harm at bay. The circle is your space - welcome some and cast out others. The circle is symbolic of ourselves. Think of personal boundaries as a magic space. Banish those that do you harm (or intend to). When you find yourself being mistreated, either directly or vicariously through others' being harmed, ask yourself if you would do magic in a magic circle with the transgressor. If the answer is "no," then examine whether than individual (or group, etc.) has a place in the magic circle of your life.

In magic, we cast the circle to establish a safe environment, where the energetic forces that we are working with are included and everything else is excluded.

Casting a proper circle takes practice. You need to have the ability to hush all the everyday thoughts, focus and draw in the energies being evoked. If you are new to circle casting, I recommend that you practice the technique below a few times before doing the cord cleansing ritual.

The Circle of Seven

Think of yourself as both a source of energy and a conduit for it. You summon the energies through concentrating on them. In True Magic we engage the four elements and the three realms. The more you understand their energy, the easier it is for you to call them to mind and to connect with them.

Our circle is cast a bit differently than usual because of the seven energies. Standing in the center of your space, in front of your septagram altar, envision yourself at the center of the star. All seven points radiate out from you. One point extends down from your feet into the ground. One point extends from your crown to the Upper World (like The True Magic Meditation). At your heart center, where the two worlds meet at the Middle World of actions, all four cardinal points (with their associated elements) come together. The Middle World (and self) is the nexus of all points. That is you in the center. The elements form the circle around you, and the Upper World and Under World pull in down into the earth and up to the heavens.

Casting the Circle of Seven

Begin with a ritual cleansing and ensure the space is tidy. If you are would up or distressed, start with The True Magic Meditation. Make sure you are in comfortable clothes. If you've got the candles on the ground, be mindful of catching them on fire with flowing garments (voice of experience talking). Arrange your altar beside an open window facing north if possible. Have your wand on the altar. You also need your written intention for the cord cleansing ritual that you'll conduct while in the circle.

Arrange seven small candles either on your altar or around you. White is fine. Begin by lighting the sage. Cleanse yourself and the area that will become your close circle with the sage. Face your altar, step back until you are in the middle of your circle.

Hold your wand with both hands at heart center. Say something like, "I cast this circle round, may only good be found and all evil be kept out." Focus on the elements, see the four in your mind's eye. Select earth then step forward. Envision the earth beneath your feet. Feel your black roots extend down as the earth rises to greet them. Call out to the element of Earth, welcoming its presence in your circle. Taking your wand in your left hand "drag" the energy of the earth with you in a clock wise quarter turn to the east (i.e. the 3 o'clock position). Call out to water from this position, add water to the earth you are dragging with you to create a half circle, stopping at the south marker (6 o'clock). Here summon Fire to your circle. Next drag all three elements to the west marker. Repeat the process for Air. Return to the north marker having completed the circle with all four elements swirling around you, lending their energy to your upcoming working and forming a firm barrier between you and the world of form. When you stepped back on the north marker, you entered the world of force.

Now, step back into your circle. Return your hands to heart center. Using your left hand, hold the wand facing down. Summon the energy of the Under World, the Lower Self and Emotion. Complete a clockwise circle drawing Under World energy into your circle, firming your boundary below.

Return hands to heart center, transfer wand to right hand.

Raise right hand up, drawn down the energy of the Upper World, the Higher Self and Intellect by completing a clockwise circle above your head. Feel the cone of power cap off your circle.

Both hands back at heart center with the wand in both hands. Say something like, "this circle is now complete."

Releasing the Circle

The process for opening the circle is the exact opposite as closing it, but we always begin and end with our hands holding the wand at heart center to lend the energy of actions to our working. Release the Realms in a counter clockwise direction, starting with the Upper World, then Under World and returning to heart center. Then release the elements by stepping to north, moving to Air then releasing it and so on until you release Earth at the north marker. At each point, envision the circle dissolving with the energies returning to their normal state. When finished, release any excess energy within yourself.

After the Circle

Note the details about the circle casting and release. How did it go? Were any of the aspects a challenge to manage? How do you feel now? These notes will help you further refine the technique. Feel free to adapt the technique to what works best for you and any specific working.

Cord Cleansing

Cleansing a relationship that serves you well but perhaps is it bit "muddied" through past hurts, normal conflicts and communication troubles is a great technique. This ritual is excellent for people you are stuck with, like an ex with whom you share a child or an annoying co-worker. Note that this is not designed for use on relationships where one person is currently engaging in warfare with the other. It's up to you to decide what relationship can benefit from the ritual.

The process is like Step 1 except the energy is of purification rather than severing. While in your circle, envision the cord between you and one other person. You can apply this spell for other people, groups and as a technique for connecting to the elemental forces in future witchery. For now, focus on one relationship.

Using the guidelines for writing a great intention from the Introduction, develop one for this ritual. Make sure you take it with you into the circle before you cast it.

Magic Seven Incantation

You can use the incantation below as part of your cord cleansing ritual that you do while within the circle. The incantation can be adapted to any working.

Hand positions to be used during the ritual: Earth and Water are left hand down; Fire and Air are right hand up. Left hand down for Under World, right hand up for Upper World. Hands at heart center for Middle World. Use your wand.

Since you have already activated The Magic Seven when you created your circle, you only need to call them to attention:

To the Forces of the North, Element of Earth,
I call you forth from below, Attend my ritual.
To the Forces of the East, Element of Air,
I call you forth from the wind, Attend my ritual.
To the Forces of the South, Element of Fire,
I call you forth from the eternal flame, Attend my ritual.

(Hands back to heart center.)

To the Forces of the West, Element of Water,
I call you forth from the water, Attend my ritual.
To Water, I call to you, give form to the Under World and the
   Realm of the Sea.

To Earth, I call to you, give form to the Middle World and the Realm of the Land.

To Air, I call to you, give form to the Upper World and the Realm of the Sky.

(Hands back to heart center.)

To Fire, I call to you, unify the forces within and without and give them form.

Elements and Realms combined in this magic circle, this ritual has begun.

Now is the time to activate your intention for a cleansing of the relational cord. Read it now. Feel the connection between you and the other person. As you infuse your intention into each of The Magic Seven, envision each one cleansing that cord. Earth will reclaim the dirt. Air will blow it clean. Fire will burn off the gunk. Water will make it pure. The Realms will remove any harmful emotions, actions and thoughts accordingly. Hold these images in your mind will you activate your intention with the following:

To the Forces of the North, Element of Earth,
Take my intention and make it so.
To the Forces of the East, Element of Air,
Take my intention and make it so.
To the Forces of the South, Element of Fire,
Take my intention and make it so.
To the Forces of the West, Element of Water.
Take my intention and make it so.
To the Middle World and the Realm of the Land,
Take my intention and make it so.
To the Under World and the Realm of the Sea.
Take my intention and make it so.

To the Upper World and the Realm of the Sky.
Take my intention and make it so.
Elements and Realms,
Released you are from this place.
The Magic Seven, I honor you.
My feelings pure,
My intention true,
And my will is strong.
It is SO!

After the Ritual

As usual, ground and then process the experience in your journal. Make notes in your BoS regarding the technique, timing, etc.

Completing this Step

The time has come to light your yellow candle. Start by lighting the black one from healing first, again taking the time to check-in with yourself, releasing any lingering resistance. Next light the yellow candle, that glimmering symbol of the light ahead and then add your wand. Acknowledge the completion of your work on relationships and boundaries.

Further Reading

Books

Relationships and witchcraft: Christopher Penczak, *The Witch's Heart.*

Ancestors: Paul Davies and Caitlin Matthews (Eds.), *This Ancient Heart*

Witchcraft Must-Read: Starhawk, *The Spiral Dance.*

Blogs

John Beckett, Why I Still Cast Circles and Call Quarters: http://www.patheos.com/blogs/johnbeckett/2017/10/still-cast-circles-call-quarters.html

Gwion Raven, Casting A Circle – Creating Magic space: http://www.patheos.com/blogs/thewitchesnextdoor/2016/07/casting-a-circle-creating-sacred-space/

Lilith Dorsey, The Hardest Thing About Creating an Ancestor Altar:

http://www.patheos.com/blogs/voodoouniverse/2016/10/the-hardest-thing-about-creating-an-ancestor-altar/

Sovereignty

I am healed from my past experiences
I am healed from painful past relationships
I am healed, my True Self is free
I am healed, I approach all things with love
I am healed, I think and speak my truth
I am healed, I act for my highest good
I am healed, I am connected to my Guides and Divine Source.

I am healed, I walk the path of acceptance, sovereignty and fierce love.
This is the way of truth,
And I claim it now.

As within, so without.
As above, so below.
This is so!

Starting this Step

I like to set up a space with the correspondences, symbols and other images associated with my current area of study. If you follow the Keeping Her Keys blog, you've probably seen some of my very non-traditional creations. For me, this focuses my energy on the concepts that I am working with. I usually make an "installation" apart from my altar in a private space. I add things that go with the concept in my mind and commonly accepted ones. Another technique for this type of contemplative altar is to create a collage on poster board. As you go through each of the Steps, I urge you create a similar space to help you unleash your Inner Witch. Creativity is everything in True Magic.

This step is all about standing in your own personal power. As a witch, it is both your right and your responsibility to fully embrace your sovereignty. We explore different aspects of sovereignty expanding upon the original the witches' pyramid to include the Under World and the Upper World, yielding the Seven Witches' Principles. Concepts explored include independence, freedom, confidence and power. As a tool for developing our ability to transform other emotions into these, I describe the practice of transmutation using a visualization meditation technique.

The major working for this step is the Sovereignty Ritual that includes several components: the Sovereignty Sigil, the Sovereignty Oil and the ritual itself. I love the process of developing a magical oil such as this and I hope you will, too.

The correspondences for this step reflect the attributes we want to draw out from us as we activate our sovereignty. The number three is associated with beginnings, balance, discipline, life, protection, life and success. The healing and relationship work from the first two steps combine with the energy of your sovereignty work to produce a new beginning.

Waxing Moon

Now we explore the returning moon. As the waxing moon increases in size, so does our ability to draw upon its growing size to attract that which we seek. In this step, it's sovereignty that is our goal. Before we move onto attraction magic, I wanted to briefly explore transmutation, so I've included a meditative technique to help develop your skills in this area. While the technique can be practiced anytime, starting it during the transition period of the dark moon, gives an extra boost of dualistic energy.

The Elements and the Worlds

The four elements and three energetic worlds are the forces utilized in this step. The four elements (air, earth, fire and water) are part of the energetic realm of the Middle World, combining with our Middle Self to complete a pyramid. This figure extends up to our Higher Selves and the Upper World and down to the

Under World and our Lower Self. We are the pyramid, emanating all the energies and interacting with their external version.

This step is the last one connected to the Lower Self and emotions. Of course, emotions play a role in subsequent chapters just as our actions and thoughts were part of our healing and relationship work.

Correspondences

Purple is the color of royalty, associated with the element of water and the crown chakra. Characteristics associated with purple include: accomplishment, awareness, freedom, personal development, sovereignty, transformation, and wisdom. **Three** is a number of rebirth, more complex than the pure energy of one, three represents combining two existing forces to give birth to something new. Think of your sovereignty as the combination of your Inner Witch merging with True Magic to fully stand in the power of your true self.

Botanicals

Two of my personal favorites are featured in this step – frankincense and birch. The properties of each of them combine very nicely together to produce the energy of freedom and wisdom. An excellent reflection of the meaning of sovereignty.

Birch

In this step, we engage birch bark. If this isn't available to you, birch essence, essential oil or birch tea can be used as a substitute. If you are using these instead of the bark, you should anoint the paper on which you place your sigil.

The dominant way that we use birch bark in this step is as its power as a binder. Birch is interesting because it can be used in removal magic (e.g., banishing) as well as attraction spells (e.g., well-being). As a binder, it can add to the power of any working. It's especially good for sigils. If you're using birch to bind anything – from your personal sovereignty to wrapping it around a poppet to remove a person from your life – be conscious of its power. In other words: be certain of what you're doing. Birch effects are almost impossible to undo.

In my experience, spells and sigils incorporating birch bark are mighty. There are supporting properties of birch that further augment our sovereignty magic: focus, freedom, protection, purification, rebirth, self-work, well-being and wisdom. Burning dried bark is a great way to cleanse a space.

Frankincense

We use frankincense as an essential oil, but it is also very wonderful in its more natural resin form. In the last step, Unity, frankincense's "cousin" myrrh is used as a resin. I love resins, but I thought that introducing you to the unique properties of this exotic botanical would be best in as an essential oil. If you want to obtain it in resin form, you'll need to grind it using your "poison" mortar and pestle. Frankincense should not be consumed. Personally, I often include it in my ritual baths because it really attunes my entire being for witchery. If you're new to it, start with a few drops.

Additional Botanicals and Substitutions

An alternative to birch for sovereignty work is juniper and/ or rosemary. The former is associated with beginnings, learn, prosperity, purification, transformation and well-being. If frankincense is not available to you, feel free to substitute benzoin and its "cousin" storax. They are resins as well. Use them in their oil form or in their natural state. You'll need to grind them in your mortar and pestle. Rosemary is quite a diverse herb. For sovereignty, you can turn to this common kitchen cupboard resident for support in focusing the mind, protection and well-being.

Stone

Amethyst which can be varying shades of purple, from deepest violet to mauve, is the stone for this step. Associated with the element of water. Properties of amethyst are like purple, including: balance, focus, the mind, protection, rebirth, transformation, stability, strength and wisdom. All important aspects of standing in our personal power.

If amethyst is not available to you, I suggest carnelian as a substitute. It is associated with personal power, the mind, overcoming obstacles, protection, success, well-being, wisdom and wishes. You can also combine this with amethyst to place on your personal sovereignty altar.

Tarot

You can include Tarot cards in your contemplative altar or vision board for this step or add them to the bag that you keep the sigil in. For your daily practice, you can contemplate cards associated with sovereignty such as the three's and the princesses (or pages depending on your deck). The Emperor and Empress are cards to meditate on to activate sovereignty. You can also work with your personal Significator card to guide you on your exploration of what sovereignty is for you. If you don't already have a Significator, selecting one now is a good way to start your sovereignty journey. It's the card that you feel most reflects your Inner Witch/True Self.

If you don't work with the cards, but use another tool such as runes, explore the themes of personal power associated with your preferred one. Not working with any sort of divinatory tool is perfectly acceptable. I'm a big fan of the cards, so I write about them a lot. Not everyone is drawn to this type of work. Don't force it if you're not.

The Bell

Bells have been associated with magic throughout history. In

Wicca, a hand bell is often included on the altar. I use a bracelet of bells from India to cleanse space and to call forth energies. You can use whatever type of bell is most comfortable to you. The bell should be cleansed in salt using the process previously discussed. You can then smoke it using sage. In the sovereignty spell at the end of the step, you'll use the bell to summon the elements and the realms, as well as attune your seven energy centers. You can practice with the bell before doing the ritual if you're new to bell magic.

If using an actual bell isn't practical for you, feel free to use your headphones to listen to a bell tone. During ritual, you can "hear" the sound while using a hand movement of ringing a bell.

Transmutation

The ability to focus on a simple object and mentally change its properties is a basic magical skill. Developing your prowess at this can be very useful when you are trying to do a ritual or spell and don't have the exact botanicals or stones that you feel are most appropriate. You can connect with the objects' properties to transmute them to align with your intentions.

This is deep energetic work, I recommend that you start with a simple color change transmutation exercise using imagery and then progress to small squares of colors. Note that the overt color may not change a great deal due to dyes and processing. However, the piece of paper will feel very different. You can test your efficacy by placing transmuted color squares in black bags, mixing them up and then blindly labelling what color is in the bag. This is a bit of party-trick magic, but it does help to hone your ability to projectively transmute the properties of an object. Once you are comfortable with the colored squares, progress to relatively simple stone and then onto plants. For the concepts of sovereignty that we explore, you can "transmute" feelings that are contrary using the technique outlined below.

Because I know you're an ethical witch, I trust that you won't run off and try this technique on unsuspecting individuals. However, the technique can be useful in certain interpersonal situations, especially for simple interactions. Think of it as good persuasion.

Technique

Begin with the mental transmutation of an orb. Hold in your mind's eye a completely black orb. Study the orb. It is black all the way through. Solid. Will the orb to change to yellow. Envision the molecules of the orb transforming. Take your time with this. Repeat the process until the orb turns to purple. Practice this a few times a day until you can do it automatically and then move onto transmuting other things. You can use this technique as part of The True Magic Meditation. Record your trials, including the objects used and the results in your BoS.

The Seven Sovereign Principles

Think of sovereignty as your personal declaration of independence. The concepts of sovereignty explored in this step are awareness, confidence, discipline, freedom, integrity, power and strength. The elements are located within the reach of the Middle World and Middle Self. I've also added the physical centers associated with each part. We use these in the anointing component of the Sovereignty Ritual. You can also refer to the infographic at the beginning of this step. I've included the Latin term for you to use as well.

To be silent (Tacere): Discipline, the direction is north, and the body location is the chest.

To know (Noscere): Awareness, the direction is east, and the right wrist is the corporeal location.

To will (Velle): Strength, the direction is south, and the

location is at the navel.

To dare (Audere): Freedom, west is the direction and the left wrist is the energy point on the body.

To go (Ire): Power, the location is the center of all energy points representing the Middle World and the corporal nexus is the heart center.

To feel (Sentire): Confidence, the direction is down for the Under World which we symbolize with our feet.

To believe (Credere): integrity is the concept, the direction is up for the Upper World and is reflected in our crown.

Awareness (To Know)

As a witch, a vital part of sovereignty is to be aware of your own internal processes and those in your environment. Of course, awareness also means that you have a considerable knowledge base that you use to exercise your sovereignty. Thus, "to know" (noscere) is connected to awareness.

Knowledge is much more than "book learning," it includes our awareness of internal processes and environmental factors. As a witch, your awareness of the world of force is part of your knowledge.

The first two steps helped you increase your awareness through healing and exploring the interaction between others and ourselves. Awareness is much more than these things, it requires developing our understanding of the forces that we work with, how we are influencing by them and how we can focus our attention. Witchcraft requires us to be able to take our awareness of a myriad of things and narrowly focus on the energies under consideration. The transmutation practice will help sharpen your awareness of the properties of objects while the emotional reversal technique you learned earlier demonstrates how awareness of feelings can help us change them.

The ideal state for magic is that of calm awareness. Our ability to reach this place is strengthened through regular meditative practice. The balancing technique outlined after this section will help increase your awareness of your corporeal being, internal state and energetics.

Confidence (To Feel)

Standing in our power requires a great deal of confidence. It helps to be a little bit cocky! With our feet firmly on the ground, we reach to the heights of mysticism and to the depths of our feelings. Thus, "sentire" (to feel) is associated with our confidence. Witches have long stood on the margins of society, wandering the woods, brewing their potions and avoiding unwarranted attention. That took a lot of confidence. If confidence is something that you've struggled with, I recommend making a list of all the things you are good at. If there are areas you feel shaky in, but feel they are important to your sovereignty development, then make a list of them as well. Contemplate the first list, really activating the confidence you have in these areas. Then taking the list and your feelings applying them to the list of areas where you feel not as sure of yourself. The sovereignty oil can be designed to activate your confidence. More on that later.

Discipline (To Be Silent)

Witchcraft requires discipline. We develop this through study and practicing techniques, such as circle casting. Part of this discipline is knowing how to use silence to reinforce our sovereignty. We may be silent regarding our witchcraft as a means of self-protection. Guarding our magical secrets is often considered part of sovereignty as well. Our knowledge is the source of our power thus we may protect it to consolidate our sovereignty. Discipline is also required to mind our own business, another aspect of silence. There is also the discipline of silencing the mind, learned through meditation and other practices.

Daily practice of the Witches' Hour of Power activities develops your discipline. If you struggle with discipline in an area that you want to develop (like a regular writing practice), start small with five minutes a day dedicated to the task.

Freedom (To Dare)

Discipline is about managing our energies, while freedom is about living a life of creativity, inspiration and independence. Freedom is a mindset. No matter what is going on in your life, you can be free. By this I mean that your approach to your external environment and internal processes can be one of freedom. You can view your responses to everything as your choice. Sovereignty means functioning from this position of internal freedom of will.

Freedom requires daring, whether it's taking the position of having a sovereign mind in a world where many choose to let others control them (including their won shadow self). There is also daring in living your own truth, which is an act of sovereignty and incredibly liberating.

Integrity (To Believe)

What is integrity? It is having a code of ethics and living up to them. Our beliefs in our own personal code are part of being sovereign. The boundary work helped you to develop "policies" for what you can tolerate from others. Integrity also is found in believing in magic, however you define it. Witchcraft requires belief that is beyond what most people can comprehend. Have integrity in your beliefs, whether it is by being quiet about them or by being an advocate. Work on developing your own "Code of Beliefs and Conduct" to activate your sovereignty in this area

Power (To Go)

If you are beginning to shift towards personal sovereignty, then your power is very much in the active stage as your energy transforms from weakness to strength. Step further into your power now and in the ritual at the end of this step. If you are resistant to do this, explore through journaling why you feel this way.

Witchcraft requires confidence in your power to bring about change through spells and other workings.

Strength (To Will)

The final principle is strength. All the six previous ones are interconnected and combine to create our strength of will. Dogged persistence is often necessary when we are learning magic. We must try things again and again until we can understand them. Witches have had to possess strong characters throughout history. As a sovereign witch, recognize that it is your will that fuels your strength. Practices such as object transmutation develop your skill at transforming your will into action. That is true strength.

Living the Witches' Principles

In your journal, write about one of the seven Witches' Principles per day for a week (or however long it takes you to get through them all.) On the first day, rank your sovereignty on each of the seven. Where do you need to turn your attention to development? What are the areas that you are already sovereign in? When exploring one of the individual constructs, give examples of when you demonstrated sovereignty in the area and make plans for how to increase your sovereignty.

The True Magic of Sovereignty

Witchcraft requires us to manipulate the natural energies around us and enter altered states of consciousness. There are times when, in an altered state, we travel to the energetic realms. Moreover, when working with herbs, stones or other correspondences we summon our own internal magic and blend it with external forces. When we engage in metaphysical activities, such as divination or spiritual journeying, we enter an altered state of consciousness. Learning to maintain our sovereignty during these activities is perhaps the most important aspect of witchcraft. This is especially true for those who have great innate magical abilities. It's vital that we learn to control our personal state of being to maintain sovereignty during and after magic. Just like in everyday life, we need boundaries or else we risk getting swept away on the energies that we summon and the metaphysical spaces we enter.

Another threat to our sovereignty comes from the energy of other people which is why we focused on the energy of others and how we manage it in Step 2. Witches are often highly empathic, so that we easily pick up on how others feel. We also often have a natural tendency to want to heal others because we can feel their suffering. Being empathic is a true blessing, but we can't walk through life soaking up everyone's energy. Plus, unless we're asked for help, it's none of our business. The same techniques that we employ to maintain sovereignty when we make magic can also be applied to maintaining our boundaries with others. In addition, developing these skills help when we get overwhelmed by our own energies. Those times when we are stressed, wound-up or spiralling with our thoughts. As witches, we have an abundance of natural energies – emotional, cognitive and behavioral – that we can learn to control and use for our own best interests. Living a magical life helps to focus our energy overall, but there are certain skills that can really train us to be better at managing our internal forces. There are simple techniques that we can learn that help us manage our magical connections, enforce personal boundaries and become better at controlling our internal states, thereby ensuring our personal sovereignty.

Balancing

Balancing refers to the practice of maintaining and restoring a sense of calm awareness that is necessary for effective witchcraft and personal sovereignty. Being balanced means that we have an internal equilibrium that is known to us and that we can return to at will. A regular meditation practice is the best way to become more balanced in general. Meditation develops our mind so that we can quickly return to a balanced state when out-of-whack. Self-reflection helps us to determine what this equilibrium means to us; therefore, writing is so important to sovereignty. Although the Witches' Principles are designed to help you activate your sovereignty (and thus life a balanced life), how you interpret and apply them is very much up to you.

While balance overall is a complex process requiring self-study and continual review, the technique of balancing our energies can be simple. There are many ways of accomplishing a balanced energetic state, but the basic premise of them all is to create a state of calm awareness. Meditation that seeks to quiet the mind is a great way to master this. However, the first step is to develop an automatic self check-in process. This is vital prior and after any magical working, but also is so beneficial in our everyday lives.

Self Check-In

As sovereign witches, we want to develop our ability to be automatically aware of our internal states, thoughts and feelings. A simple self check-in practice consisting of regularly pausing for a few moments before beginning any new activity helps. Ask yourself:

- How am I feeling? Am I hungry? Tired? In pain?
- What am I thinking? Are my thoughts swirling?

- What do I need to accomplish this next activity?
- Is this in my own best interest? If not, how I can make it so?

Adding these practices to your Witch's Hour of Power is a great way to get in the habit of doing the balance check-in. You can add a "balance evaluation" as part of your daily writing practice. What areas do you feel balanced in? Where are you out of sorts?

Binding

One of the basic parts of witchcraft is our ability to attach things together. In creating the sigil, you'll bind the sigil to birch (or paper). Binding can refer to containing energy within an object or a person, or to creating an energetic cord between us and something else. We're using it the third way – to solidify magic.

Binding needs to be carefully considered. When properly done, binding is very challenging to undo. Binding is generally considered a type of removal magic because it "ties" an object for a specific purpose. Within a removal perspective, all obstacles are removed when the object is bound. But, it's also attracting in the sense that is compelling two forms together. Just like we can work with dualistic lunar energies during the Dark and Full Moons, we can engage correspondences using two opposite types of magic in one spell or object.

Binding is often done to remove a harmful object (including people) from a witch's life. However, binding can be done to tie together objects, such as people in a relationship, as done in a hand fasting ceremony, or ingredients in a spell. In the sovereignty sigil exercise, we bind our personal emblem onto a piece of birch bark (or paper). Other binding botanicals include: mandrake, thorn apple (American mandrake), and skullcap.

Sovereignty Sigil

Making your own personal "power sigil" is a great magical

undertaking to activate your sovereignty. Creating the sigil is a fantastic journey of self-exploration. You'll be surprised by the things you discover! Once the sigil is created, you will use it in the ritual at the end of the step. Fully charged, you can carry it with you as a "secure base" that you can connect with when you feel your sovereignty start to waiver.

Preparing to Craft the Sigil

The process requires a couple of pieces of birch bark (or high-quality paper), a purple marker (and other colors that represent you) and paper to develop the sigil. You can "attune" the birch bark for a few days prior to putting the sigil on it by keeping it in a non-opaque black bag with the piece of amethyst. Velvet is a good choice of fabric for containing the energies. I suggest blocking off about three hours for creating the sigil.

Crafting the Sigil

Your sovereignty sigil needs to reflect your personal energy in a very powerful manner. There are many ways to go about selecting what to include in your sigil. Laura Tempest Zackroff's *Sigil Witchery: A Witch's Guide to Crafting Magic Symbols* is an excellent resource of sigil magic. Something else I do is use the Greek letters. You can also use your astrological considerations of sun sign, moon sign and ascendant. If you don't know these, you can get them for free from astro.com. You'll need your birthdate (including time) and location.

Favorite symbols, flowers and other things can be incorporated in the sigil. I recommend working with the name you call yourself (mundane or magical). Research the meaning if you don't already know it. Study all these things associated with your name, but also include the seven Witches' Principles by incorporating the symbols of the elements and realms as you feel led. Craft a sigil that is as powerful and unique as you!

Technique

There are many ways to reduce symbols, letters and numbers into one sigil. My favorite approach is to study the images for common simple shapes, like lines and circles. I draw these beside the image. Once I've done it for all the words, etc. that I want in my sigil, I look for the commonalities. For example, if you name is "Tyler" and you're using Air, Saturn and Leo in your sigil, then you would reduce the letters in the name and the symbols down to lines (vertical, horizontal and diagonal) and basic shapes (circle, triangle). The "y" and the triangle for air can be layered on top of each other as part of the sigil. The horizontal line in the capital "T" can be used as the shaft of the sigil, with the other symbols resting on it or around it. You may use the symbol for Leo or even your numerical birth date.

Remember that this is your sovereignty sigil. Incorporate the symbols that speak power to you. Sketch out your sigil until you're happy with the design. Then copy it onto the birch bark using purple as the base color. Add additional colors as you wish. Store the sigil in the bag with the amethyst. You'll activate it with the sovereign oil that you'll make next.

Sovereignty Oil

The next step in our sovereignty witch-crafting is to create a unique power oil. You'll use this oil to activate your sovereignty both in body and in the sigil (which is an extension of you). There are many ways to create your sovereignty oil:

By blending together simple essential oils. ("Simple" refers to an oil with only one botanical ingredient).

Creating a concentrated oil.

The process for blending simple essential oils is straightforward. You can use your sun sign, moon sign and ascendant. If you use essential oils, as you add each one into the blend, recite the incantation. Recite the incantation (more on that below) over the oils at ninety-minute intervals over the course of one full day. You'll need a small lidded jar to keep them in. You can take the amethyst out of the bag and place in the completed oil. In addition to the frankincense, which really activates your power, add botanicals that reflect who you truly are. Here are some associated with the astrological signs.

Aries	Chili powder, juniper, mushroom
Taurus	Cumin, apple (blossom), lovage
Gemini	Rose, mugwort, frankincense
Cancer	Daisies, chamomile, alder
Leo	Bay laurel, peony, sage
Virgo	Lavender, peppermint, walnut
Libra	Geranium, verbena, hawthorn
Scorpio	Basil, dill, ash
Sagittarius	Dandelion, rowan, juniper
Capricorn	Moss, magnolia, holly
Aquarius	Fennel, curry, wisteria
Pisces	Jasmine, nutmeg, pine

Crafting a Condensed Oil

I offer the above guidelines for blending essential oils to make your own sovereignty one in case you aren't comfortable with some witchin' in the kitchen. Either approach will do, although the concentrated oil will be much more powerful since it is your own unique creation. I firmly believe that the most potent magical creations begin with basic ingredients that we craft ourselves.

The contents you select for your own oil can be selected from the list of astrological signs and botanicals.

You can use dry or fresh botanicals, or a mixture. If you are adding essential oils (or essences made with alcohol), ensure that they are safe to heat. Or you can add them to the finished product. You can easily use the botanicals already on hand: ginger, yarrow, sage, frankincense and leftover birch bark if they speak to your personal power.

Frankincense will combine with your chosen ingredients to create a super charged sovereignty potion. If you are making the concentrated oil (instructions below) add that after the warming process is complete, then blend saying the incantation while doing so.

Crafting Powerful Incantations

Always write an intention whenever creating a magical product, like this oil. Refer to the guidelines in the introduction. After you write your intention and select your botanicals, it's time to write the incantation that you'll say over them.

Starting with your intention in the center, construct a new word web in your journal or other notebook (unless you record everything in your BoS) that includes the botanicals you've chosen, the elements in your sigil and the seven principles. I use my journal or scrap paper to write the incantation until it is polished and then write in the Book of Shadows. When you record it in here, you can select inks that correspond to your spell. This is one flourish that I always do when recording an incantation. A great added boost comes from adding a bit of magical water to your inks.

You can write a script that includes the various things you'll be doing during the spell and other directions beside your incantation. The script for this working is the process for preparing the concentrated oil (described below.) I usually have the incantation and then the instructions underneath of it. For an incantation to be effective, you must include your own plans for manifestation. Be specific in what you're asking each of the botanicals to contribute to your sovereignty.

Tips for writing an incantation

- Connect the words with correspondences.
- Use active language. Follow the same rule that I strive to in all writing:
  Strong verbs. Short sentences.
- Choose words that directly relate to the type of spell.
- Be consistent in the energy of the words.
- The structure of the incantation contains energy, too. Using rhyming techniques will enhance the energy of the spell.
- You can build an acronym reflecting your intention into the incantation to make it even more potent.

Once you've written the incantation, it's time to prepare the concentrated oil (or blend the essential ones together).

Concentrated Oil

Making a concentrated oil is a completely different process than an essential oil where costly equipment extracts the natural oils in a botanical, such as with the resin of frankincense. Our oil uses warmth to expel the botanical's psycho-spiritual-physical properties gently into the fixative based (in this exercise, I recommend using high quality organic olive oil). What is yielded is a type of infusion. Contrast this method to making a tonic using boiled water where the properties of a botanical are forcibly released by heat. A gentle diffusion made through a long period of warmth captures the botanical properties without activating them all at once. Think of it as a "slow release" versus a "quick fix."

Supplies

Clean 750 ml mason jar (1 quart)
Tools: pot with lid (small enough that there isn't a lot of "air space" between the 3 cups of oil and the lid)

Mortar and pestle
Witch spoon
Knife for chopping if using fresh ingredients
Cheesecloth or fine mesh strainer (for removing ingredients)
Small bottle for carrying oil once prepared
Purple cloth and string for covering the oil

Ingredients

Fixative oil: 2 cups high quality organic olive oil
Botanicals: Refer to table or of your own selection. ¼ tsp. each
for ground botanicals. 1 cup each for fresh ones.

Process

This oil takes one full day to prepare. Start in the morning.
Gather your ingredients. If you can, harvest them yourself. I've
included botanicals in the table that are easily found in gardens
during the spring and summer. Light your work candle to cast
out unwanted energies. Envision your space protected by the
energy of the candle. Assemble all your ingredients. Gently heat
the oil until it is warm to the touch. Don't let the oil get hot or
boil; that will result in it burning off, destroying its ability to
absorb the plant matter.

If you are using dried botanicals, grind them thoroughly in a
pestle and mortar first in a clockwise manner. Gently combine
the herbs with the warm oil. Cover. Leave the heat on a very
low setting, maintaining the warm to the touch temperature. I
recommend leaving the heat on for intervals of five minutes,
then cover the pot with a cloth and remove heat. Although there
shouldn't be any actual steam, the oil will give off heat, resulting
in some vapour that could escape if the pot isn't well wrapped.
Repeat this process for 12 hours. The constant warmth will
permit the slow release of the botanicals' properties. Recite the
incantation each time you warm it. At bedtime, wrap the oil well
for the night, reciting the incantation again as you put your oil

down for the night.

In the morning, strain off the botanicals and pour into the Mason jar. You can reserve a bit to test on your skin for sensitivity and to "get to know" while the jar of oil sets. Add the amethyst. Seal the jar. Get the purple cloth and string ready. Pour a few drops of wax from your work candle on the center of the lid, place the cloth over it and then tie it around. As you tie, recite the incantation one last time. Place in windowsill for a minimum of three days.

Sovereignty Ritual

The goal of this ritual is to fully activate your sovereignty. You will emerge from it fully standing in your own power. Preparation includes the usual cleansing and purification. If you can, wear purple during the working. You've already created all the supplies you'll need, although you can add purple candles if you like. You can pour the oil in a purple bowl or another one reserved for the oil. Alternatively, you can funnel it into a small vial (don't use clear for storing oils for longer periods). Remove the amethyst and have it on standby. Have your oil and sigil ready at your altar. Shamanic drumming with a medium tempo works well.

This ritual is best done while laying on your back, although you begin standing. Assemble what you'll need to feel comfortable while in this position.

Creating Magic space Using Bells

The left hand should be used to shake the bell for the Under World, earth and water. The right is for Upper World, air and fire. Raise your arm for summoning the Upper World, lower it for the Under World. For calling the elements, your arm should roughly be at heart center (the Middle World position). After you light the candles, you are ready to begin.

Focus on the elements, see the four in your mind's eye. Select earth then step forward. Envision the earth beneath your feet. Feel your black roots extend down as the earth rises to greet them. Connect to your emotions and the energy of the Under World,

Shake the bell once using your left hand with it pointing down to the ground:

To the Under World and the Sea,
My Lower Self and the energy of emotions,
I call upon you now,
Attend my ritual.

Switch the bell to your right hand, raising your arm up. While doing so, concentrate on the energy of the Upper World and the power of the mind. Shake the bell once and say:

To the Upper World and the Sky,
My Higher Self and the energy of intellect,
I call upon you now,
Attend my ritual.

Hold the bell in both hands at heart center. Focus on the Middle World and the energy of actions. Shake the bell once and say:

To the Middle World and the Land,
My Middle Self and the energy of actions,
I call upon you now,
Attend my ritual.

Maintain the height of heart center for calling upon the elements.

Facing north, call out to the element of Earth, welcoming its presence in your space. Shake the bell in your left hand, then say:

To the Forces of the North, Element of Earth,
I call you forth from below, Attend my ritual.

Turn to the east, shake the bell in your right hand (heart center level)

To the Forces of the East, Element of Air,
I call you forth from the wind, Attend my ritual.

Turn to the south, shake the bell in your right hand and say:

To the Forces of the South, Element of Fire,
I call you forth from the eternal flame, Attend my ritual.

Turn to the west, shake the bell in your left hand and say:

To the Forces of the West, Element of Water,
I call you forth from the water, Attend my ritual.
Elements and Realms combined with the Selves and Functions,
lend strength to this working.
This ritual has begun.

Anointing

This consists of activating your sovereignty, the sigil as a representation of your sovereignty and attuning the two. If you have skin sensitivity, you can either anoint your garment or the air just in front of the appropriate location.

Pour a dab of the oil on the index finger of the appropriate hand at each point in the ritual with the same positions from the bell casting. As you work through the steps, envision the cord the runs through you from the Under World to the Upper World. This transects your Middle Self/World at its apex. The four elements extend down from this creating a pyramid around your Middle Self. Refer to the infographic at the beginning of the step for the corresponding colors. You are the purple pyramid that grows forth from this center and draws in the energies of the elements.

Stand for this part of the ritual. Once you are anointed, lay flat on your back. Begin with the bottom of the sigil and your feet, representing the Under World, emotions, the Lower Self and the concept of "Sentire."

Anoint your feet saying,

Sentire, To Feel.
My feelings are sovereign and reflect my truest self.
Confidence is mine.

Anoint the bottom of the sigil saying,

I attune my sovereign emotions to this sigil.

Raise your right arm anointing your crown, saying

Credere, To Believe.
My mind is sovereign and reflects my truest self.
Integrity is mine.

Anoint the top of the sigil saying,

I attune my sovereign mind to this sigil.

Bring your hands to heart center, envision the top of the pyramid. Anoint your solar plexus, saying:

Ire. To Go.
My actions are sovereign and reflect my truest self.
Power is mine.

Anoint the middle of the sigil saying,

I attune my sovereign actions to this sigil.

Using your left hand, anoint your chest saying,

Tacere. To Be Silent.
Discipline is mine.

Anoint the corresponding point on the sigil saying,

I attune my discipline to this sigil.

Using your left hand, anoint the area under your belly button saying:

Velle. To Will.
Strength is mine.

Anoint the corresponding point on the sigil saying,

I attune my will to this sigil.

Anoint your left wrist, saying:

Audere. To Dare.
Freedom is mine.

Anoint the corresponding point on the sigil saying,

I attune my freedom to this sigil.

Anoint your right wrist, saying:

Noscere. To Know.
Awareness is mine.

Anoint the corresponding point on the sigil saying,

I attune my awareness to this sigil.

Holding the sigil and the amethyst, lie down. You can turn the music on at this point if you haven't already. Make yourself comfortable. Place the sigil at your solar plexus with the amethyst on top. Feel your physical being and your ethic entity as a unified whole. What works for one does so for the other.

Work through each point of sovereignty following the same sequence used in the anointing. Feel the oil activating the associated concept. Filling your being and attaching to the sigil. Take your time at each point, letting messages come through.

When finished, return to your physical being gently. Wiggling your toes and fingers. Rise slowly. Release the magic space:

Elements and Realms, I release you now.
This ritual has ended.

Place your sigil in the bag, along with the amethyst. Sleep with it under your pillow. Then carry with you. Whenever your sovereignty is threatened, connect with the sigil to restore it. If the threat is strong, the sigil may become depleted. In that case, repeat this ritual. Should the sigil feel completely exhausted, make a new one. Anoint yourself with the oil on the seven points for the next few days. Also use it to restore your sovereignty after a rough day. You can use this oil to prepare altar tools and other objects of great personal power as well.

After the Ritual

Record your experiences, including the messages you may have received. Be extra gentle on yourself for the rest of the day. Be prepared to have dream world adventures in sovereignty the night following the ritual. You may want to keep your journal by your bedside.

Completing this Step

After finishing this ritual, update your altar with the purple candle for this step during the Step Completion Ceremony. Light the candle from Step 1 first, using it (if possible) to light the second one and so on. Replenish your goblet with fresh potion with a few drops of your oil mixed with living water or a favorite wine. Anoint your wand and chalice with the sovereignty oil at the end of the ritual (once it is activated). Claim them as your powerful tools of True Magic.

Further Reading

Blogs

Heron Michelle, The Paradox of Personal Sovereignty in Modern Witchcraft. http://www.patheos.com/blogs/witchonfire/2018/03/paradox-personal-sovereignty/

Lilith Dorsey, Love Crystals: Amethyst http://www.patheos.com/blogs/voodoouniverse/2018/03/love-crystals-amethyst/

What is Frankincense? **https://blog.mountainroseherbs.com/what-is-frankincense**

Cyndi Brannen, Don't Tell me What to Think: My Beliefs are as Valid as Yours. http://www.patheos.com/blogs/keepingherkeys/2017/12/my-beliefs-are-as-valid-as-yours/

Laura Tempest Zakroff, The Power of the Quiet Witch. http://www.patheos.com/blogs/tempest/2018/05/the-power-of-the-quiet-witch.html

Books

Laura Tempest Zakroff, *Sigil Witchery: A Witch's Guide to Crafting Magic Symbols*

Devin Hunter, *The Witches' Book of Power*

Scott Cunningham, *The Complete Book of Incense, Oils and Brews (Llewellyn's Practical Magic Series)*

Arin Murphy-Hiscock, *The Green Witch: Your Complete Guide to the Natural Magic of Herbs, Flowers, Essential Oils, and More*

Growth

Spells, like life, are a combination of everything that's already been added or experienced. In this way, they are an ever-expanding spiral with each new step representing exponential expansion. All of life is such, including our actions, thoughts and emotions. At the crossroads of the Middle Self where all forces manifest, we can choose to expand ourselves or stagnate. Growth mindset is a powerful way of approaching life and witchery.

Starting This Step: Witches' Hour of Power Review

Before we begin this step, I want to talk about the Witches' Hour of Power for a bit. I based the idea for this transformative approach to magical and personal development on the convincing science showing that dedicating one hour/day to such things leads to dramatic improvement in all areas of life. Of course, I witched it up by including magic as one of the activities. Don't forget that daily practice of The True Magic Meditation counts as part of the Witches' Hour of Power. Other activities include writing and daily Tarot practice.

The goal for the amount of time you spend on your Hour of Power should be one that makes sense for you. The Spell of the Seven Fires at the end of this unit is an excellent framework for strengthening your Hour of Power Practice. You can choose one practice to activate through the spell.

One of the key secrets of True Magic is to build in success when starting a new practice. Set small goals that you are likely to achieve. This is a sort of risk reduction. You'll be less likely to become discouraged and more apt to succeed. Maybe your hour only has five minutes before bed and five in the morning. If this is what makes sense for you, then don't stress about not doing a full hour. Use the Spell of the Seven Fires to really activate your Hour of Power practice.

What is this spell you ask? Before I get to it, we've got a lot of ground to cover. Let's begin!

New Moon

The Spell of the Seven Fires should be launched on the New Moon. If you want to add to the activating ritual of the spell, you can call down the moon at the beginning. True Magic involves both using the natural ebbs and flows of the lunar cycles as well as intentionally drawing them down into our workings.

The Energy of Fire

Fire energy can be intimidating. It's natural to be wary of it. I think this valid fear stems from seeing fire as only a destructive force, and that it's something that we can't control. Fire is like witchcraft itself – wild, but manageable. Skill and confidence are necessary to control both. Fire is also like our actions – how many people do you know who go through life without putting much thought into what they do or how they live? But since we're here together, neither one of us is that sort of individual. I love playing with fire, but I have a healthy respect for it. Fire is part of my everyday life – from burning incense to bonfires. If you are timid of working with fire, be gentle with yourself as you move into this step. Find ways of increasing your comfort with fire energy that are appropriate for you. For example, you can burn a few scraps of paper in a stainless-steel sink. You could even write "I am no longer afraid of fire" on the paper before burning it to create a simple removal spell.

If you can't use with actual fire, use battery operated candles instead. Remember that all electricity is borne from a spark, so there is always fire inside any electrical device.

Correspondences

Red, as a representation of fire and of the blood that symbolizes the Middle World/Self, is our major color for this step. Since we are using fire energy, yellow and orange can be added if you wish.

Red is the color for the full moon and action. Black represents the Dark Moon, with white for all the phases in between. It's a little bit tricky to think of the Full Moon as red since it's usually white. However, the energetic color of any object can be different than the perceived color. Contemplate what the full moon means to you and what it represents to understand its inherent redness. I'll talk about the colors of the moon in the next step on connection where we get into the energetic properties of the Three Realms more.

Red works well for witchery about assertiveness, creativity, passion, protection, strength and truth. This is also the color of the crossroads.

There are two numbers to contemplate. The number **four** is about attraction, creativity, focus, protection, stability and well-being. For our purposes, we can consider the four-way crossroads where we are at in this step and when we function from the power of our Middle Selves. Here at this juncture we meet the four elements, themselves a crossroads of energies.

Since you'll be doing the Spell of the Seven Fires at the end of this step, seven is an important number to contemplate, especially as you develop your seven-part plan of action for the spell.

Botanicals

The three recommended botanicals for growth are chamomile, orange peel and olive oil. All associated with different aspects of fire, they combine to form a great source of gentle, sustained and strong magical energy. You can blend them together using the concentrate oil technique from the last step, make a tonic or mix them in your non-toxic mortar and pestle.

Chamomile is a dry, fiery plant. Think of it like well-seasoned wood, it will produce a warmth that is slow and steady.

Chamomile is well-known for its calming ability. Properties of chamomile include: attraction, determination, grounding, growth, patience, purification and success.

Orange can be employed in a variety of different ways – from the juice to the blossom. Orange juice is well known to promote a general sense of well-being, but did you know that it is also good for activating your intuition? Interesting bit of orange juice lore.

Drying orange peel:
Using a sharp vegetable peeler, scrape off the outer peel only (avoid the white pith, it stinks when burnt). Chop the peelings into small pieces. Arrange on parchment paper. Bake at 200 for 25 minutes (until dry to the touch). Let cool. Store in an air tight container. Kept in the fridge, this will last three months. Blend with the chamomile for a tonic of grounded growth – warming fire from chamomile and brighter flames from orange. ½ tsp of each.
Properties: attraction, creativity, growth, prosperity and success.
Make a candle holder by carving out an orange to add strength to growth spells. Pack inside the orange with botanicals associated with your working.

Olive Oil was used in the last step to make the sovereignty oil. I encourage you to use chamomile and orange to make the same type of oil for your growth magic.

Properties of olive oil are many: abundance, balance, consecration, healing, prosperity, protection, purification, rebirth, success, wealth, well-being.

When using olive oil as a base, don't forget to include its properties in your working, such as summoning the energy in your incantation.

Uses: As a fixative, for consecrating candles and tools, for anointing and for burning in lamps. NOTE: olive oil has a low burning temperature compared to some other oils, so watch the heat.

More on Botanicals

Orange peel can be replaced with other citrus peels or cinnamon. Chamomile can be replaced with another gentle but powerful warming herb such as thyme. Blackberry can be added to make a potable potion that inspires growth. Ensure that you focus the energies of the plants while brewing this. Steep a handful of the berries with a teaspoon each of chamomile and dried orange peels in boiled water for about five minutes. You can also make a vinegar from this. Olive oil can be substituted with high quality almond oil. You can make a concentrated oil for growth using the technique in the previous step.

Stones

You can make an amulet from a piece of **red jasper** for growth, using the techniques from the citrine one in Step 2. The way we work with it in this step is as a touch stone for the Spell of the Seven Fires.

Red jasper is an excellent addition to workings about focus, energy, grounding, healing, optimism, protection, prosperity, strength, well-being. An alternative or additional stone for growth work can be malachite if you want to try something different. It is a complex stone for growth magic, especially for shifting your energy away from the past towards the future. Another way of looking at this is to move from the Under World of emotions towards the celestial energy of intellect. All the stones used in previous steps can be incorporated into growth witchery. Obsidian removes barriers, citrine clears the way, and amethyst attracts.

Tarot

If you work with Tarot Cards, you can study the Fours in

conjunction with this step. Temperance and The Chariot are also beneficial to meditate on.

The Blade

The blade is forged from fire. Like fire, it is a composite of other ingredients, unlike the other elements or the other tools. In Tarot, the Suit of Swords is most often associated with air, but there is a long traditional of it being representative of fire. I think it's a personal choice and suggest that you interpret any Sword card in relation to your working or the adjacent cards in a reading. Wands work the air, but does the blade work the fire? Wands can be destroyed in fire...but a blade is borne of fire. I'll leave this up to you to sort out. For this step, the blade relates to fire.

The blade is also deeply symbolic of growth. We chop food then combine with other ingredients to yield a complete dish. The birth knife is used to cut the umbilical cord. Plants and trees need to be cut back for maximal growth. The knife cuts forms and shapes used in magic.

The blade is the most complex tool as fire is the most complex element, so is the Middle Self/World. So follows growth, an interplay of various forms and forces. All have the potential of creation and destruction. I liken the blade to my own powers – I can cut things down to destroy them or I can sever my connections to things that no longer serve. When we chop up ingredients, we are breaking them down to create something greater than the sum of each one.

I often use the blade to cast the circle, to pull in energy and to be my "stand in" for various rituals. I have a blade I use exclusively for this sort of energetic work, but I wouldn't hesitate to use it to cut objects if it felt appropriate. The blade as an extension of ourselves can be worked with in many ways. I've included its use as a reflective surface in our fire scrying exercise.

If you're interested in a Wiccan understanding of the blade, I've included a book on the athame in the Further Reading section. I have a very distinct approach to the ritual use of a knife which is very different than mainstream pagan practice. When arranging your altar at the end of this step, you can place the blade in the southern position to represent fire. You can use the Wand Correspondence Quest to acquire a new one, although you'll be hunting in the retail world instead of nature. I add charms to my blade to correspond with different things, like the seasons or special workings.

Understanding Growth

Ground is the key word for this step – our feet (and the rest of us) are firmly on the earth for the work ahead. Think of this step as a crossroads, where the four elements and realms meet to create the Middle World. This is where we bring force (thoughts, emotions, energies) into form through our actions. We are always anchored to our physical being even when we temporarily leave it to explore the etheric worlds. Thus, our Middle Self is the constancy of our human life. Its expression, our actions, are the product of all the forces. As a result, this is the most complex realm and self. The Middle World exists as a form and force constantly. Contemplate the energy in all the objects surrounding you right now. How many of them are comprised of natural products like wood or glass? Is there electricity being used to run them? Electricity at its foundation is a type of fire. It's also the "life blood" of the devices that we depend upon. Like our blood, electricity is a living thing that fundamentally bends towards expansion as does the entire universe.

Growth is the natural condition for all things. Yes, we go through periods of stagnation, decline and death. But the motivator is growth. If our blood is pumping, we have drives to eat, drink, learn and do other things. When we lose this propensity, we often are very ill or become sick because we've lost our "spark."

The Witches' Hour of Power is about practices that ignite

that spark. I wanted to give you an opportunity to use spellwork to enhance this practice, so I developed The Spell of the Seven Flames from traditional candle magic. Everything I talk about in this step builds towards this working.

The Spell of the Seven Flames is of the Middle Self and Middle World because it is about translating the forces (of emotions, thoughts and elements) into the form of our actions. The spell is about growing something new. Spells, like life, are a combination of each previous ingredient (or experience). In this way, they are an ever-expanding spiral with each new step representing exponential expansion. All of life is such, including our actions, thoughts and emotions. At the crossroads of the Middle Self where all behaviors manifest, we can choose to expand ourselves or stagnate. Growth mindset is a powerful way of approaching life and witchery. Part of this is accountability. I hope you take the time to do the journal activity on accountability to yourself and others.

Growth Mindset

My youngest son and I were talking about growth mindset while I was writing this section of the book. It's become a popular tool for empowering learners. He groaned when I brought up the subject, saying that he's grown enough. He was kidding. He also said that one of the key concepts of growth mindset is also a joke among his friends. The power of "yet" is central to a growth mindset, as in "I can't do this" being replaced with "I can't do this...yet." He said his friends take all sorts of ridiculous statements and then add "yet," like "I can't eat 117 sandwiches...yet." While this sounds like a fun game, it also points out that growth mindset should be applied to realistic goals and expectations.

True Magic requires a growth mindset. The belief that we can get better, that our abilities can improve, and our intelligence increase are the hallmarks of a growth mindset and powerful witchery. Of course, this comes with the caveat found in my sons' joking about "yet." We need to match our spell work with what is possible for us to achieve. Grasping beyond our reach results in ineffective spells. Know thyself is truly the most important rule of witchcraft. Being aware of our limitations and strengths is part of being accountable for our actions. Accountability, being responsible and trustworthy is vital to successful relationships with others. More important is that we hold ourselves accountable for our own actions, including the spells we cast. Thinking back to the Seven Witches' Principles, you can see how growth mindset naturally flows from this model. Thus, growth mindset is both the continual growth of ourselves tempered with understanding our limits. The energy of a growth mindset combines with our witchery to yield True Magic. I want you to really contemplate the items below.

Features of a Growth Mindset

- Acquiring knowledge is a positive experience
- Everyone can learn
- Self-determines outcomes
- Embraces challenges
- Others' success inspires me
- Learn from feedback
- Effort is a path to mastery
- Makes plans with measurable goals
- Works at goals every day
- Accepts responsibility
- Persists despite setbacks

Characteristics of a Fixed Mindset

- Learning is hard and painful
- Everyone but me can learn
- Other forces control outcomes
- Avoids challenges

- Jealous of others'
- Ignore advise and criticism
- Effort is a waste of time
- Makes grand statements without actionable steps
- Procrastinates unnecessarily
- Blames others
- Gives up easily

Journal prompt: Explore the characteristics of growth and fixed mindsets. What are ones that you are strongest in? What about the ones you need to "grow?"

The Meaning of the Middle Self

A growth mindset is very much about our actions. It's about pushing our limits so that we become more authentic and sovereign. When we think about the Middle Self, it's easy to see that growth is the fundamental force at work. While it's true that we often stop doing things, or change our ways, our natural inclination is to replace them with new ones. Like the universe, we are always expanding. I've talked about the Middle Self throughout this step, how it represents the coming together of the Worlds and Selves and the crossroads connecting us to the elements. The Middle Self is also on the receiving end of all these energies. Therefore, everyday practices, like in The Witches' Hour of Power are so important for not only your growth but also protection from these energies. As your authenticity expands, you can accidentally radiate so much energy that undesirable forces (and people) get drawn to you. Having your boundaries established and sticking to them is also very important. Don't forget to reinforce them from time to time.

The Power of Actions

Since the Middle Self is the expression of our forces (emotions and thoughts) and the filter through which we interact with the world, a great exercise is to play with the energy exchange of the Middle World by doing something out of the ordinary. Of course, witchcraft is unusual in and of itself, but intentionally playing with accepted norms through specific behaviors is an exercise that can teach us about the volatility of the energies of the Middle World. When I taught Applied Social Psychology, I had the students go out and do an exercise where they had to violate a norm. This could be something simple like standing the wrong way in an elevator or more striking like literally laying down on the job. For this exercise, you should do the same. Pick a safe behavior that is short, easy to do and that will let you observe both your own reactions and that of others. Do this on your own without involving anyone else. It's best done with strangers or at least people you don't know very well. Trust me it doesn't take much to upset the natural flow of the material world. Even walking the wrong way in a crowd is going to cause a reaction within yourself and others. Being so bold as to do a disruption activity is definitely an act of your Sovereign Witch.

Write about the experience afterward and then contemplate how this simple and brief mundane activity (which can cause such a temporary disruption) can be applied to the forces that you manipulate using magic.

Centering

After doing the disruption exercise, it's a good idea to get your energies back in order. Grounding and balancing do this, as does centering the technique I'm introducing now. Exercises that develop our mindfulness skills through meditation, balancing, grounding and centering, reinforce this force by helping us retain our sovereign power.

Centering helps us to achieve the optimal state of calm awareness using our physical being. I use centering often because I tend to get completely up in my head, ignoring everything below my neck. Not only do I get more stressed when I do this,

I tend to ignore basic bodily needs like eating and going to the bathroom! Being centered is a core skill for magic as well. When we create intentional awareness of our own physical state, the benefits are many, including:

- Increased consciousness of our bodily needs
- Naturally diminished desire to do harmful things to our bodies
- Awareness of the power of our bodies
- Connection to this power to use in magic

Technique

Stand with your feet hip-width apart. Your arms should be relaxed at your sides, with your gaze straight ahead, fixed on one point. Turn your attention to your feet. Is there tension in them? Relax them and spread your toes. Evenly distribute your weight between the balls of your feet and your heels. Bring your attention up through your calves to your knees. Again, check for tension and release it, slightly relaxing your knees. Continue with this up to your trunk. At your heart center envision a cord running through your body down into the earth and up to the sky. Is this cord straight? Correct your posture as necessary to straighten it out. Continue with the relaxing technique up through your shoulders, neck and down into your fingertips. Then pull that calm awareness up to meet the same in your mind. When doing any sort of working, you should start by ensuring that you are centered by checking in with this cord. Of course, you need to be balanced and grounded as well. When your working is complete, do the grounding if required and check-in with that cord.

Form into Force

The social disruption exercise demonstrates that the world of form – actions and material things – deeply influences the word of force – emotions and feelings. You may have even left a shift in the energy of the location where you did your little act of social rebellion. The Spell of the Seven Fires at the end of the step is designed to help you do this sort of disruption in your own life over a sustained period, to yield lasting results. You may experience changes in the attitudes of others towards you and in the overall energetic climate of your home. Make sure you keep an eye on these things, but also enforce your boundaries and use those communication skills to explain why your Witch's Work is so important to you.

While the disruptor exercise demonstrated how a mundane activity (form) turns into changes in emotions and thoughts (forces), it's also helpful to contemplate how the material objects we work with in magic are activated as forces. Botanicals are material creations that are imbued with properties that we release in different ways, by decocting them in boiling water, by burning them, etc. In their natural state these properties exist, but we release them into the world of force through specific techniques that are themselves based in the Middle World and conducted by the actions of our Middle Self. Plant properties are both chemical and spiritual. The properties associated with any botanical is usually the result of eons of lore and scientific research. One system organizes these properties with the dominant energies of the planets. Other perspectives, like shamanism, structure their understanding differently. The more you work with botanicals, the more comfortable you'll become extracting their forces from their forms.

Creation and Destruction Magic

Before I talk a bit about transforming the form (material symbols) of the elements into forces, we need to consider the two basic types of all magic: creation and destruction. All growth is preceded by a time of destruction, from quiet fallow times to the chaos of a storm. Thus, is fire, that which burns all clean but also gives us heat, enabling life and light. Fire cannot exist without the other elements, another way that it is more complex than the other three. I typically categorize magic as being on a continuum from attraction (creation) to removal (destruction).

Fire Scrying Using a Blade

Fire scrying is a time-honored practice used in many ways in witchery. You can use the reflective surface of your blade to add a different dimension to the practice. The basic technique is to enter an altered state and then focus your attention on the fire. You're already well prepared to enter a trance; you can use the counting technique or chanting. You want to be in a light trance where you are open to metaphysical forces but are still aware of your surroundings. I suggest using a black candle, although a white candle will work in a pinch and you could use a red candle to scry specifically about what you are growing in the spell in the next section.

The room should be dimly lit, to minimize distractions. Light the candle on your altar prior to beginning your chanting. You can burn some of the sage or place a few drops of frankincense on the candle to augment the experience.

While you light the candle, say something like, "Fire, fire burning bright, grant me insight on this night." If you have a specific issue that you want to explore, concentrate on that. If not, open your awareness.

Holding your blade in your dominant hand place it behind the candle so that you see your reflection and that of the candle in the blade. Steady the blade by holding the tip with your other hand. You can rest your elbows on cushions or a table. Look past the candle into the blade while chanting. Take note of any images that come up and record them in your journal later. The combination of the magic flame with your chanting can lead to strong visions coming through. By looking into the blade, we shift our attention away from the direct flame to the energetic field that surrounds the candle and merge it with our own image. You'll soon begin to perceive images form in the space between the blade and the flame. Don't be concerned if images don't appear instantly, remain relaxed and they will come. If your mind starts to wander, dismiss your thoughts by telling them that you'll see them later. If you're new to fire scrying do this exercise for about five minutes. When you are finished, thank the fire for lending its energy to your work. Be sure to journal about the experience. You may also want to record the technique in your Book of Shadows.

The Spell of the Seven Fires

I've been hinting about this spell throughout the entire step. Now it's finally time to get into it. The supplies are quite simple, though the technique is complex.

Supplies

Chamomile

Orange peel

Red jasper (bag to carry it in if you wish)

Seven small candles (like votives or long-lasting tea lights)

Platter or tray – gold/fiery looking (about 16 inches will give you enough room to create the fire spiral)

Tools

Blade (for extinguishing flames and creating/opening circle)

Time: New Moon

Overview

This step has been all about growth within the context of our Middle Self/World. I've talked about how growth requires us to become uncomfortable. We don't grow by staying still. We need to change up our actions to ensure that we continue to develop.

In the disruption exercise, you had the opportunity change one specific activity. Here I give you The Spell of the Seven Fires as a ritual to activate and support a longer period of intentional growth.

The spell is designed to be active for six "segments" with the seventh being the completion of the spell. The first part includes the first step plus the activation. The final step is to "solidify" the spell, end its active period and "cement" the growth you've experienced. The process of the spell and the associated activities will lead to real growth. Having that seventh week also gives you built in extra time. Remember that being accountable requires us to set realistic intentions that are actionable in the Middle World. Building in extra time is responsible spell casting.

This is a complex working, although the ingredients are few. I wanted to introduce the idea that complex spells consisting of straightforward correspondences and methods often yields fantastic results. The opposite approach, simple spells with complex correspondences and methods is fraught with risk. A spell needs to be carefully constructed. Think of it like a fire. If you just throw a bunch of stuff together and try to light it with once match, it'll probably not burn. If you throw fire starter (complex ingredients) on any pile of things, it'll burn but you won't be able to control the outcome. You want a well-made fire in a proper container than you can control. Once a spell is spoken, undoing it is very difficult.

Focus

You can choose any action that you want to grow. I recommend picking one of the Seven Witches' Principles or a practice for your Witches' Hour of Power. You are moving force (concept) into form (action) using form (fire and correspondences) to release their forces (their energetic properties) to support your work. The spell will support you will you are growing during the six weeks. Think of it as a spiral that activates your intention, but also gently gives your energy to keep going. Growth takes a lot of energy. Chamomile and the olive oil provide sustained release support will the orange peel gives an instant boost. Lighting the candles activates fire energy and the shape of the spiral "spins" the spell to life.

If you are working on specific goals rather than a time frame, adjust the spell accordingly. However, I urge you to connect these outcomes to a date to help keep yourself on track. If your goals will take longer than a week, that's fine.

Once you have chosen your concept, develop your intention. The next stage is to make a plan for the six weeks, sort of a mini-intention for each one. I recommend writing these all on separate sheets of paper.

You can add additional correspondences if you like, but the only required ones are the color red, fire, the golden spiral, chamomile, orange peel, olive oil and the red jasper.

Once you are happy with your intentions, write an incantation that addresses each one plus the one for solidifying the spell (i.e., week 7). The first part should address the activation (initiation) of the spell and include what you will do the first week. Each subsequent week will be about that week's focus.

Example

Concept: To develop a disciplined daily witchcraft practice.

Goal: 20 minutes/day average on magic by the end of Week 6.

Intention: To easily find more time to spend developing my magical practice with no harmful consequences and that this will greatly increase my witchy abilities.

Sample Schedule:

Week 1 spend five minutes/day practicing mental transmutation

Week 2, review Week 1. Expand transmutation to 10 minutes or add five minutes/day to a new magical practice – creating enclosed magical space (i.e., circle casting)

Week 3, review Week's 1 and 2. Continue in these practices, expanding by five minutes or add new activity, such as connecting with my blade.

Week 4, review Week's 1-3, either continue and expand by five minutes or add new activity, such as connecting with a symbol of one of the elements.

Week 5, review and expand time on earlier practices or add five minutes of trance work (free form dancing is great for this).

Week 6, review and expand time on earlier practices or add five minutes of drawing down lunar energy.

You've reached 30 minutes/day. Remember this is your average, same days may have less or more.

End of Week 6 complete the spell. Solidifying all your work.

Incantation

I wrote this incantation in a broad way, so you can adapt it to your focus. However, you can write your own from scratch if you wish. Since this is a highly personal spell, the more of yourself you put in, the more likely you are to manifest what you desire.

I often use numbers in the incantation when it's a spell that has distinct components.

By the fire of 1, this spell's begun. (light first candle)
Witch I am, so witch I'll be.
Grant me the time and energy.
On Week One, _____ shall be done.
Come Week Two, all shall come true. (light second candle)
Adding more time and skills new.
Growing stronger in my craft, on the third week, (light third candle)
I'll further expand.
Daily practice makes me stronger,
On Week Three, time spend grows longer. (light fourth candle)

By the fifth week, new discipline grows, (light fifth candle)
Adding more to all that I know.
Week six finds me doing more, (light sixth candle)
As new abilities I explore.
Now the spell has come to pass,
I light this candle to make the effects last. (light seventh candle)

Preparation

The usual process of preparing the correspondences, objects and tools should be followed. If you are using your blade for the first time, make sure it's been properly attuned to your energy after purification. Sleeping with a knife can be tricky, but you can place it in a safe space near your bed. Spend about five minutes each day connecting to its energy until it feels like a natural extension of you. Decorate your knife however you wish if you haven't done so already.

The herbs and the oil will be on the tray for six full weeks. I recommend changing them each week before you do the candle lighting.

Set the altar tray up, arranging the seven candles into a golden spiral (i.e., the space between each candle gets bigger). Get the botanicals ready. You can either blend them beforehand or not. If you're also making a tonic and/or the oil, then it's easier to mix up a batch in your non-toxic mortar and pestle.

Using the botanicals in more ways always adds strength to any working (as long as this is done properly). You can drink the tonic and/or anoint yourself with the oil daily or once a week when you do the candle lighting ritual. Alternatively, you can carry some in a red bag (or one with a fire symbol on it) with the red jasper to use as your secure base to connect with the spell when there are challenges to meeting your goal.

The Circle

I recommend adapting one of the earlier methods using your

blade instead of the wand or only your hands. Make sure you note any differences after the ritual.

Casting the Spell

Since this spell lasts for six full weeks, you'll activate it during the initial casting and then once/week for each week until you reach the completion at the end of the sixth week.

Activation

This is the initial lighting of the Seven Fires. Recite the incantation, light each corresponding candle and then sprinkle the botanicals to link each candle to the next (completing your spiral). If using dry herbs, place them first and then anoint with the oil. If you've made the concentrated oil, you're all set. As you work your way through the incantation and the activation of the correspondences, envision yourself doing the activity for each week. See how each activity causes your focus to grow exponentially. When you light the seventh candle, use your blade to create a spiral in the air above it (do this with your dominant hand).

Now it's time to extinguish the candles. Keep in mind that you are putting out the form of the flame, but not the force.

Start with the final candle: "This flame I release." And so on.

With the final candle to be put out (i.e., candle #1) add: "My spell is cast, the energy is released. May all come true and all barriers cease." Or something like that.

I like to finish here with kissing the blade to seal the spell within me.

Release the circle, do the processing and get busy growing!

You can do the fourth candle lighting ceremony on the altar after you complete this part of the spell. Add you blade to the altar after the candle is lit.

Weekly Ritual

At the end of each week, light the candle for the upcoming one. Use this as a time of reflection for how the previous week went, to decide what your focus will be for the next week, etc. Change the herbs/oil and re-arrange your spiral. Start by lighting the first candle (Week 1 is done, the spell's become), then lighting the second one (Week 2 is new, the spell's come true). You can replace this chant with the different weeks or use your own. When it comes to the seventh candle, light all of them in sequence from 1 – 6. At each lighting, take time to reflect upon what you did that week. Envision the skills and knowledge you've accumulated being solidified deep within you.

Light the seventh candle, "This spell's complete, no meagre feat. Let all that's done, never be gone." Or something like that.

Take your blade and in your non-dominant hand create a counter clock wise spiral drawing the energy of the spell down in the last candle. Snuff out this candle with the blade and then each subsequent one. If you've successfully closed the spell, you'll feel a sense of completeness, and probably a bit drowsy. The growth process is demanding. Since you've just completed an intense period of learning, you may want to schedule this final ceremony for an evening when you don't have big plans for the next day. Take it off, then move onto your next project. Regular rest periods are as important to magic as activity.

Dispose of the candles and botanicals. Cleanse the platter/tray for future use.

Record and process.

Finishing This Step

Light the fourth candle on your altar after lighting the previous three. I like to use each candle to ignite the following one. Place the blade on your altar while contemplating its ability to bring forth growth.

Further Reading

Blogs

Mat Auryn, Your Ego is Holy. Available at: http://www.patheos. com/blogs/matauryn/2018/03/23/ego-holy/

From IFL, Examples of the Golden Ratio You Can Find in Nature. Available at: http://memolition.com/2014/07/17/examples-of-the-golden-ratio-you-can-find-in-nature/

Sorita D'Este, The Unification Rite (Elemental Magic). Available at: http://www.patheos.com/blogs/adamantinemuse/2017/12/unification-rite-elemental-magic/

The Witches Next Door, A Ritual for the Elements: Magic You Can Do. Available at: http://www.patheos.com/blogs/thewitchesnextdoor/2017/08/elemental-ritual-elements-magic/

Books

Carol S. Dweck, *Mindset: The New Psychology of Success*

Mario Livio, *The Golden Ratio: The Story of PHI, the World's Most Astonishing Number*

Jason Mankey, *The Witch's Athame*

Starhawk, *The Spiral Dance*

Connecting

Being able to open ourselves to others and experiences is vital for all connection whether to those we care about or to our animal allies. To get more specific, openness can be associated with each of the Three Selves. Connecting with and developing our Higher Self requires an open mind. Fundamentally, this is about belief in ourselves, others and magic. If you don't believe that witchery is real, you'll never open up to it.

Starting this Step

Continue your work with the Seven Fires Spell. Since the step is about connection, there is an emphasis on opening up, which requires us to become vulnerability when not properly protected. This is a good time to revisit your boundary work from Step 2. Also ensure that your sovereignty work is remaining strong. Keep adding to your Witches' Hour of Power.

The scope of this step is quite different from the previous ones, reflecting the energetic shift towards the refined, mystical air of the Upper World. Our journey has taken us from the Under World, the power base of all witchery and practical magic towards mysticism and magic (or high magic if you prefer). In the next step, we stretch even higher with an introduction to astrological correspondences. This is a good time to review the characteristics of the Three Worlds, especially since we journey in the Liminal Realm in both a ritual and in lucid dreaming in this step. I've included a detailed table in the back of this unit with loads of information about the Three Worlds to help with your understanding and spellcrafting.

Setting the Tone for this Step

When starting your journal section for this step, make an infinity loop on the center of the page. Around it label all the things to which you feel connected in a beneficial way. On the second page draw another loop and list all the things that you would like to be MORE connected with. As you go through this unit, review this list with each new skill you learn. How can you apply the concepts, practices and techniques to becoming more connected? In the next step on Abundance, I'll be talking about color magic. You can go back to this infinity loop exercise and add appropriate hues then. It's ALL about connection.

Waning Moon

The energy of the waning moon is added to our mystical journey to the Three Worlds to remove all blockages.

Energies

Here we begin the transition to the more refined, mystical timbre of the Upper World, but we are still grounded in the Middle World and the elements. We voyage to the Other World where the energy can be emotional, action oriented or purely intellectual. In general, we go into Other World work from an intellectual more Higher Self approach, but our time in the Other World in this step is a blend of action and thought, whether in the Lucid Dreaming exercise or our animal spirit journey.

Mercury

Mercury as a god and planet is very much the energy of communication. In this step we turn to Mercury's planetary energy as a way of understanding the role of connection in all forms of communication. Mercury is associated with blue, the number five and the goat (which is the animal guide in the journey). Mercury is also about unencumbered communication which the goat guide will ensure. Mercury is also associated with visions. Add the Mercury symbol to spells of communication, connection and openness. It's a stick figure with two small horns.

Correspondences

Blue is the color for this step, representing communication which is the essence of connection. Blue is associated with the astral realm, or the Other World, where you'll travel for the animal spirit journey. It's also associated with awareness, intuition, protection, truth, visions and Upper World wisdom. It's also connected to mugwort one of the botanicals for this step and is the color of the type of agate used.

The number five is associated with blue. Properties relevant for this step include action, communication, connections, protection, spirits, and travel (you'll be journeying to the Other World). Five also represents the pentagram, the combination of the elements and ether (aka "everything else"). It is the number of the original witches' pyramid. While we harness the four elements, there is often the fifth element – the everything else – added to them. You can think of the Three Worlds as all that ether.

Botanicals

In the last step we used relatively simple botanicals but in more complex ways, the opposite is our approach for this one.

Mugwort

The witches' best botanical friend, except for some who have an allergy. While rare, it does happen, particularly in those who have a ragweed allergy. If you are new to working with mugwort, make a weak decoction and rub it on the inside of your arm to test for sensitivity or burn a bit if you can. Mugwort can be burned, consumed (in small amounts for a short period of time), smoked (if you're so inclined) and used in other ways. In this step, I am introducing you to making a poultice for psychic activation.

Properties: psychic abilities, astral realm, animals (it will help keep unwanted animal attention away on your journey), dream magic, messages, power, protection, rebirth and visions.

Oak

I'm using the mighty oak to introduce the use of tinctures, also known as essences. These can be made at home. However, they require 75% proof alcohol and the process is challenging, so it's easier to purchase them. Bach's flower essences are the best brand to buy. The great thing about using tinctures is that most of them are safe to consume in very small quantities. They can also be applied to the skin without concern unless there's a sensitivity. These are two characteristics that essential oils don't offer for our herbal crafting. The alcohol increases the potency of the botanical properties, making them a good alternative to oils.

You can also chop up fresh leaves for use in this step. You can make your own concentrated oil of mugwort and oak using the instructions from earlier.

Properties: shamanism, rebirth, purification, protection, energy, healing, independence, power, spirits (animal and nature), wisdom and witchcraft.

Alternatives

Olive oil can be used as a fixative in a psychic opening oil or on its own for anointing your third eye. You can mix it with, although the experience won't be as powerful compared to the mugwort and oak combination. If you tend to respond strongly to psychic activation, consider adding a bit of yarrow to the mugwort and oak poultice used in the journey to keep you grounded. This will yield a deeper connection. Yarrow is especially good for animal magic and spirit contact, so it's most suitable for the journey. For something different, if you are adventurous, explore the ways that cedar opens you up to the plant/stone spirits in this activity. Cedar is great for psychic ability, summoning spirits, protection, purification, and rebirth.

Stone: Blue Agate

Banded blue agate is ideal, although other types of blue agate are fine. This particular type of agate is best for visionary magic, such as the Three Worlds Animal Spirit Journey in this step. All blue agate is great for communication enhancement. You'll be using the agate as a communication conduit in the journey at the end of the step. There are many types of agate. I've included a link in the further reading section if you are interested in learning more.

I usually offer one or two alternatives, saying that they will work almost as well. Not in this case. Banded blue agate is the perfect stone to use as a connector in the journey. If you want to explore other stones, I suggest making an energy grid consisting of amethyst (psychic ability), red jasper (protection) and aquamarine (visions, protection).

Tarot

The Lovers is a great card for contemplating connection. The fives are all about transformation, so they will help you open up. The High Priestess or the Magician (traditionally shown with an infinity symbol over his head). The Fool is all about being open, so that connection can occur. I suggest doing a five-card spread with the following structure: Card 1 – Opening the Lower Self, Card 2 – Opening the Middle Self, Card 3 – Opening the Higher Self,

The Feather

You can use whatever type of feather appeals to you – a large one from a bird of prey or a collection crafted together from smaller birds. Like the blade and the wand, the feather is an extension of your energy and a conduit to the external ones represented by the tool. You can go on a feather quest, something I have found to almost always be successful. Of course, you can order ones either plain or decorated. Add charms to your feather how you feel led. I have used a turkey feather which is a bit of an unusual choice for Higher Self and Upper World energy for years. It's from my ancestral farm, so it has deep connection with who I am. I bound the end of the feather with the traditional witches' colors of black, red and white.

> *Light as a feather.*
> *Gift of flight.*
> *Magic*
> *I call to me,*
> *On this very night.*

You've cast the circle with your hands, wand and blade, so you've probably already figured out that I am going to suggest you do the same with the feather. You can use it to cast the space for the animal/stone spirit connecting exercise, to create an energetic container prior to your lucid dream work or before preparing the psychic patch (more on that later) for the animal spirit journey.

Openness and the Three Selves

The Higher Self, being at the outermost tip of our being, is not a place where we want to reside in our daily lives, however, we should draw from its wisdom, thus returning to that place of balance in the Middle Self. For our shamanic journey at the end of the step, we will be activating our Higher Selves and Upper World energy. It's good to do a lot of lower level of connection magic prior to this, so that your skills are well honed. This is why there are two "warm-up" exercises in this step – the plant or stone animistic exercise and the intentional lucid dreaming activity. We don't want the animal spirits we encounter to possess us, we want to be open to receiving their communication through our connection.

The Importance of Openness

Being able to open ourselves to others and experiences is vital for all connection whether to those we care about or to our animal allies. To get more specific, openness can be associated with each of the Three Selves. Connecting with and developing our Higher Self requires an open mind. Fundamentally, this is about belief in ourselves, others and magic. If you don't believe that witchery is real, you'll never open up to it intellectually even if you heart very much wants you to. Hope is the characteristic of an open heart. Although we use the heart center as the physical location for our Middle Self, it's important to remember that feelings very much influence our actions. When we close down our emotions, not only do we deny our Lower Selves their full experience but our actions – especially in terms of relationships – suffer and are typically dysfunctional. Finally, openness in the body describes a sense of physical freedom in the Middle Self. It is the desire to move more and in new ways.

Stagnation and Vulnerability

When we are shut down to all that our Three Selves, the material world and magic has to offer, we stagnate. This is characteristic of having a fixed mindset. This is when the shadow self is running our lives. Our Inner Witch is chained. The risk in openness is that we become vulnerable to all sorts of things. This is where our boundaries and sovereignty become so important. We are much less vulnerable when our energies are true self based rather than shadow driven.

Curiosity is a way that openness is naturally expressed by our Higher Self energy. Creativity is a great way to open your Lower Self more. Think way back to the beginning of this book when I asked you to make an altar featuring a septagram. It was an exercise in openness, creativity, self-expression and maybe you learned a bit about the magic of the septagram, connectivity in all things and color properties.

The exercises in this unit will help you expand your experience, knowledge and skills in the world of pure force. Dream work and shamanic journeying are often purely force based exercises. In this step, we incorporate material world objects in our Other World magic, utilizing their energetic properties on "the other side." Doing these activities helps to deepen our connection to the Other World but can also be "touch stones" for drawing us back in our Middle Selves. Most of the ingredients we use in witchery have both force and form. Contemplating the openness in plants and stones, who also have Three Selves is another way to open ourselves to specific connections, but to hone our general skill at magical communication.

Opening the Middle Self

I mentioned earlier that new actions help us to connect to our Middle Self through our physical bodies. Time to let your Inner Witch play! To practice opening the Middle Self up more, I recommend adding five minutes a day for a week of a physical activity that you rarely or never do. It should be something that engages your full being. Dancing is an easy one, but you could try running or even walking backwards! Start by creating a page in your journal where you list all the physical activities you already do, then listing ones you'd like to try and simple five-minute ones that you can easily accomplish. Consider this part of your Witches' Hour of Power. Do the activity in a mindful way, observing the changes in your Three Selves. Add a few lines in your journal each day about the activity.

The Power of Communication

From our thoughts and words to exploring plant connections, communication is the essence of human existence. Animals communicate without language, as do plants and stones. We've spent time on human verbal communication (and connection) in step 2, here we are on the other side where the focus is on different types of communication and the ensuing connection. Like with establishing boundaries and now we are pushing our openness, we are exploring the opposite end of the connection spectrum through plant, stone and animal spirit work.

The Energy of Connection

The connections between the three functions of emotions, actions and thoughts are the energies fueling our personal infinity loop. At either end are the two pure dimensions where our human abilities connected with either cease to have any material form. However, these extremes – the pure Higher Self of intellect and Lower Self of instinct funnel their energy into our functions, and likewise our functions influence them. We are in a constant infinity loop of the three functions, in any moment our actions, thoughts and feelings are co-mingling. The ability to discern what is motivating us or causing upset is a vital skill to develop on the way to your magical life. Regarding witchcraft, the ability to pick apart tangles of ingredients – whether they be our functions or spell ingredients – helps to strengthen our magic.

Mindful Moments

A mindful moment takes these practices a step further by adding brief meditation into your day. We typically use the energy correcting strategies only when we are out of sorts, but a better approach is to take the regular self-checks and add a moment of intentional breathing at regular periods throughout the day.

In a mindful moment, begin with your self-check:

What am I feeling right now?
What am I doing right now?
What am I thinking right now?

Answer the three questions, using "I am" statements. Don't include anyone else in your moment. It belongs just to you. After you answer each question, release the energy of each one. "I release anxiety," "I release the pain in my back," and "I release worrying about getting this project completed on time" are three examples. As you work through the release statements, begin to pull your breath deeper and release it gradually, blowing away the emotion, thought or physical sensation/action with each out-breath. Pranayama breathing – letting the breath rattle a bit in your throat making a bit of a growling sound – is great to add to this technique.

Botanical and Stone Spirit Communication

Non-verbal communication is interpreted through words in our human minds, but plants, stones and animals don't have words. When you sit with your chosen botanical or stone, I want you to try two different approaches with two different objects. In this first instance, choose an object purely on instinct, one that you know nothing about. In the second, research the object extensively and then connect with a specific property or two. Stones are great to connect with, but to me, botanicals will always be my preference. Plants have such great personalities and properties. Stones are inherently less connected to us because they aren't living objects, but I like using them for the convenience. It's difficult to take my mugwort plant with me in the car!

Procedure

Set aside at least thirty minutes to do the connecting. You'll want to create a closed energetic space around you and the botanical or stone. Before opening the connection, do a mindful moment or other energy correction. Then envision a cord extending from your Lower Self to the corresponding one in the object. Really open up your emotional channel bi-directionally. Let the plant or stone know you first. Good manners matter in plant and stone spirit work. Don't download though, just show the object what you're feeling. Then "ask" the object to reciprocate. Try to avoid applying words to the experience. See colors, feel emotions. Repeat this for the Middle Self, try to let the plant or stone (they certainly vibrate even though they don't move) physical properties possess your physical self a bit. Finally, do the Higher Self connection where you let your thoughts and mystical energies flow into the object and then explore the similar ones in the plant or stone. The plant or stone may transmit a message to you that you'll interpret using words, as much as you can try to avoid this. See shapes, colors, changes in air flow, light/dark, etc. from the perspective of the botanical or stone.

Botanical Connections

All plants have Three Selves, reflected in their roots, stem and blossom or branches. Their Other World is as fascinating as their physical properties, and just like with all things is very connected. I have had a deep relationship with mugwort for at least two decades, while oak is more like an occasional visitor. Perhaps like visiting royalty or a rich relative!

Use the Three Selves framework once you've connected to your chosen botanical. What emotions does the plant have? What are its actions (you may think that plants don't move, but they certainly grow in patterns and respond physically to the environment)? What are its intellectual and mystical qualities?

Stone Connections

The blue agate is a natural connector, although I find it to be more of a mediator than an actual talker. To me, it is a conduit, so it's a completely different personality than a more talkative stone. Rose quartz is very chatty and is great stone for opening the heart, while our old friend yellow citrine is great for opening the mind.

Making a Psychic Patch

One method for magical herbal crafting that I really like but is to create a poultice. Basically, a patch that is applied to the skin, botanical properties are released directly to a specific area and then travel throughout the entire body (both etheric and physical) rather than the vice versa. I like this approach for working with psychoactives like mugwort. The effects immediately go to the energetic center being activated. While it the substance is absorbed through the skin, the bulk of the effect is through spiritual connection between our energetic focal point and the properties of the plant being used. Unlike the costly "flying ointments" that have a similar effect, a psychic poultice is very inexpensive and easy to make. You only need the botanicals and gauze. You can add a stone to the decoction while it steeps it you like. I am recommending it for our psychic poultice.

Think of the psychic poultice like an ice or heat pack applied to a certain area. Another way we use a poultice is as a bandage to cover a wound. We can use them to treat holes in our auric field as well or to remove blocks.

Ingredients

Mugwort (about 1 tsp. per ½ cup boiled living water)

Oak (about 10 drops of essence or a couple of drops of essential oil, about 2 leaves shredded – if using fresh oak leaves, leave decoction steeping for an additional 5 minutes)

About ½ cup boiled living (i.e., salt, clear fresh or purified spring) water.

Piece of Banded Blue Agate is best

You can make a mugwort & oak infusion to drink as well. Use only an oak essence that is labelled as safe to consume – most of them are. Most essential oils aren't. If using fresh oak leaves, make sure they aren't from a sprayed area. Wash well before ripping up and steeping. ½ tsp. mugwort to 3 drops essence or one shredded leaf.

Supplies

100% fine cotton gauze (undyed is best if you can get it)
Kettle
Scissors
Small heat-proof bowl with lid
Measuring cup
Measuring spoons

Timing

Do this about twenty minutes before starting the Three Worlds Animal Spirit Journey. You want the botanical properties to seep into the gauze, but not overdo it. This is especially true if you are new to working with mugwort and oak.

Directions

Let gauze rest in salt bath overnight, you can include the agate if you haven't cleansed it yet.

While the water is boiling, cut an eight-inch strip of the gauze. Carefully spread the mugwort along the length of the gauze, then add the oak essence. Fold the gauze in three and place in your bowl. Pour ½ c water over the poultice. Add agate. Cover immediately. Set the timer for 10 minutes.

When the time's up, lift the poultice out with a wooden spoon. Press off all excess liquid. If you like, you can scrape off the mugwort. It depends on your experience with the plant and whether you mind bits of mugwort on your forehead. Remove stone. Begin journey immediately.

Using the Psychic Patch

For the animal spirit ritual, you should cast the circle with the feather immediately after preparing the poultice. Bring the steeping decoction into your space, while it does its thing cast the circle. The psychic patch is best used as soon as ready.

The patch is best used lying down for obvious reasons. Once

you are comfortable, place the poultice over your third eye on your forehead. Think of the poultice as an energetic lens that will sharpen the vision of your third eye. Hold the stone in your dominant hand. Concentrate on connecting to the energies of mugwort and oak, seeing your Higher Self begin to communicate with the plant, becoming more activated. Breathe deeply into your body while the poultice activates, starting with filling your lower body with air and then drawing your breath up to your third eye, finishing here. After a few minutes, you'll feel a physical sensation in your forehead and your perception of the material world will start to soften. You will feel your third eye open wide with a general feeling of openness throughout your body. You are safe in your magic space. Once you begin you'll have Goat to further protect you. All is well. All is as it should be.

Three Worlds Animal Spirit Journey

This journey is Middle World with a leaning toward the Upper World. We are through the crossroads and moving toward the heights of thought, away from action. This is a great mixture for doing this sort of animal spirit journey. The energy of the journey is primarily that of action as you are venturing through all three worlds, but the emphasis is on communication which is a blend of middle/upper energies.

This journey is about connecting to animal spirits to receive your unique words of power. One of the animals may present itself as a spirit guide. Animal spirits can be guides, where they provide advice or solely as companions where they give support but no guidance. You can have a totem which is an animal that you strongly connect to. It can be one that is very much like you or completely dissimilar.

Shapeshifting is an excellent technique to learn. I've included Ted Andrews' classic *Animal Speak* in the further reading section. You'll find a great section on practicing shapeshifting in it. For this journey, I am asking you to tell your existing animal spirit companions to take a break. You want to create the space for new ones to come forward.

However, you won't go into the journey without a guide. Goat will serve as your guide throughout the journey. Goat spirit is suitable for this journey because they are one of the few animals that can easily exist in all three worlds. Their Under World energy is as a symbol of magic. In the Middle World, they serve as domestic animals. They reside in the Upper World on the cliff tops watching over all things. Goat energy is strong and aggressive, making an excellent guide for this sort of work.

Preparation

Supplies

Psychic Patch
Blue Agate

You can hold three pearls, beads or other small tokens (black, red and white are perfect) in your non- dominant hand to offer the animals in exchange for your word of power. The agate will be given to your guide.

I recommend listening to a slow shamanic drum beat or track during this ritual. Do your research to find one that appeals to you. I am suggesting "Encounter" by Mark Seelig on his "Intention" album. It's 15 minutes long which is the average time for the journey. You can find it on Spotify.

Timing

The Waning Moon and on a Wednesday if possible. It's Mercury's Day giving a natural communication boost. While activating the poultice, envision the waning moon energy clearing away all blockages between your Middle Self and the Higher Self, see your third eye being cleansed. Concentrate on cleansing your infinity loop, fully opening your energetic selves to the adventure ahead.

Since you're moving directly from the activation of the psychic patch, there is little to do except transition into the ritual.

Journey Procedure

Goat spirit will be happy to serve as your guide especially if you offer a token. This is what the blue agate is for. After the psychic patch is activated, envision in your mind a door that leads from the material world to that of pure force. Enter through the door into the Liminal Realm. Here you will immediately meet goat. Greet him, offering your agate as a token in exchange for taking you on a journey to the three worlds to receive a word of power from an animal in each one. The agate is on a beautiful blue cord that you tie around his neck. The charged agate will help you connect with Goat to ensure your protection and success during the journey. You may notice a shift in the physical agate in your hand after you give him the token.

Envision the three worlds as the lemniscate. Here at the beginning, you are at the crossing point. This also represents the Middle World which we symbolize with the cardinal points. You are not concerned with them since they represent the material world. The "other" side of the worlds is where you're focus is on.

Spend time here in the space between worlds connecting with Goat. Let him feel your openness and trust. In return, he will extend his protection to you. When you are ready, let him know that it's time to begin.

At this point, three pearls appear in other hand, signifying that it's time to begin. The door to the Middle World is behind you, the doors to the other two realms on either side. Goat will lead you to the Under World first, while you follow him take note of your surroundings. A deep sense of trust and of being in the right place fills you. Soon an animal will appear. Offer this creature a pearl in exchange for your word. As you pass the pearl to the animal, it will transform into exactly what the animal wants (probably food). Take note of the animal's appearance, behavior and mannerisms for processing later. When the animal gives you the word, it will appear in your mind's eye. The animal may have more to say, so trust Goat to lead you away when it is time. When it's time to go, say the word aloud and thank the animal.

Now goat will lead you to the Upper World. Follow the same procedure of offering the pearl, observing, listening, saying the word and expressing gratitude. Goat will lead you back to the crossroads of the Three Worlds. You'll cross into the purely energetic Middle World where you will meet the final animal. Repeat the process.

When finished with the last animal, Goat will lead you back to the door where you can cross back into the material world. He will either ask you to take back the agate or indicate that he is to stay on as an animal companion. Thank him either way and release him from his work.

Begin the process of returning to the material world when ready. Release the agate and pearls then slowly remove the psychic patch. Steady your breath, gradually letting it return to how you typically breathe. I want to emphasize taking your time here because of the level of openness you've activated and all that you've experienced. If you find you are still really activated, release the excess energy through controlled deep breath through your nose. Draw your breath into the third eye/Higher Self and then gently close it down. You can't function in the mundane world when you are too much in the heights of the upper one. Sink back into your physical body as you release.

Process the journey as you usually do. Pay special attention to the non-verbal cues the animals gave you when they gave you the word. This is where you'll find their message for how you are supposed to use each word.

Some questions to ask yourself:

- How was the animal behaving?
- What was the animal's facial expression?
- What was the animal's posture?
- What was the animal's appearance?

Research the standard symbolism of each of the animals after you develop your intuitive interpretation. Merge the two together to find the meaning of your word and how to use it.

Using Your Words of Power

You can make a power sigil from the words to carry with you at all times. Carry it in your sovereignty bag to bind the words to you. Use the words in your spell incantations. It's really up to you how to use them. "As above so below" was given to me by Isis as my personal word of power years ago, I have it tattooed on my left wrist.

Ending This Step

I find this journey to be very intense, so I am recommending that you do the step completion ritual a day afterwards. Light the blue candle and add a bit of the mugwort and a few oak leaves. Since you are finished with the agate for now, feel free to place it on the septagram as well. Let Goat's wisdom of The Three Worlds mingle with your altar while you contemplate all that you've experienced. You can keep the agate as is to connect with goat more quickly in the future. Store in a dark blue or black bag after you complete the ritual.

Further Reading

Blogs

John Beckett, *Intuitive Animism*. Available at: http://www. patheos.com/blogs/johnbeckett/2016/08/intuitive-animism. html

Barbara Heider-Rauter, *The Power of the Infinity Symbol*. Available at: https://omtimes.com/2018/03/power-infinity-symbol/

Keldon, *Working with Plant Spirits*. Available at: http://www.patheos.com/blogs/byathameandstang/2017/05/working-plant-spirits/

Books

Ted Andrews, *Animal Speak: The Spiritual & Magical Powers of Creatures Great and Small*

Brené Brown, *Daring Greatly: How the Courage to Be Vulnerable Transforms the Way We Live, Love, Parent, and Lead*

Ross Heaven and Howard G. Charing, *Plant Spirit Shamanism: Traditional Techniques for Healing the Soul*

Eric Pearl, *The Reconnection: Heal Others, Heal Yourself*

Abundance

What is an abundance? To me, it's a magical life where the true self shines and the shadow is healing. Days filled with wonder and witchery. A content home where I can simply be. People around me who really get me. Being able to support others on their journey. And travel, I need to roam! It's having what I need to get by; a truck, a broom and waterproof boots. That's about it...oh, and books. I need lots of those. Chocolate. Finally, my magical life includes a healthy lifestyle of mind, spirit and body. I need the material resources, so all these things are sustained in the long-run, so financial stability is huge. If I've got all that, I'm good. What does your Magical Life look like?

Before Starting this Step

The ideal time to do the Magical Life Project ahead in this step is during the waxing moon. I recommend you complete the Spell of the Seven Fires before you get into the project. You will be moving from strategic growth to massive growth. The Spell of the Seven Fires is a great warm-up act for launching in the Magical Life Project.

Before commencing this step, be sure that you have thoroughly processed your adventure with goat. You can use those words of power in the incantation for your magical life spell.

The Witches' Hour of Power practices shift towards abundance in this step, so why not take an inventory of your current practices before adding the new ones of affirmations and gratitude? What is working? What isn't? If you are feeling lethargic now, I urge you to go back to the beginning and work through the ritual bath technique again. Sometimes, intense spiritual development work like you've been doing can require a period of rest. Be gentle with yourself before moving onto the abundance work ahead.

Waxing Moon

Our lunar correspondence for the actual spell part of the project is the waxing moon since the working is a type of attraction magic.

Energies

Abundance is not limited to the material world, we seek it in all areas of our lives. A few of us seek a prosperous spiritual life and reject the material world. Most of us, including myself, are not going to do that. Abundance includes prosperity in all things that are important to us as individuals. Our health, finances, relationships, activities and possessions are material things that we possess. We either lack enough quantities or we prosper. This step is dedicated to prosperity in the material world. We live in a material world even as witches who walk between the worlds of form and force, our primary residence is in that of form. As such, the energy of this step is predominantly earth elemental.

I talked about Mercury in the last step, but now I'm broadening this to include The Seven Wandering Stars. I love calling upon the planetary energies, so I've included a bit about their properties.

Correspondences

Green is the color for this step as it is most associated with the earth element and that thing we use to acquire material possessions – money. It's also the color of the heart chakra. A happy heart doesn't need to have an abundance of earthly goods, but we all have the right to claim prosperity as we define it. Other themes of green include: abundance, accomplishment, adaptability, action, prosperity, protection, rebirth, success, trusts, well-being and wisdom.

The number **six** is associated with money, balance, happiness, creativity, well-being, wisdom, life and love. I encourage you to use this number when creating the Magical Life spell at the end of this unit. You can use six correspondences and have six stanzas in the incantation.

Botanicals

Two of my favorites are included in this step – **pine and bay laurel**. I love bay laurel so much that I wrote an entire article about this multi-tasking tree. We work with the laurel leaves (think of those wreaths on the ancient Greeks heads). They can be shaped into so many magical objects beyond fancy headwear. A simple "happy home" trick is to fill a bowl with sea salt and then arrange bay leaves standing upright. You can use one leaf per household member. Bay laurel properties: abundance, manifestation, determination, prosperity, truth, success, purification, truth and wisdom.

Pine cones are associated with abundance, activation, beginnings, growth, money, motivation, self-work, transformation, truth and wealth. Pine cones are a splendid example of the Golden Spiral. Both pine and bay laurel are great hex breakers. If you are feeling cursed, make a charm to carry with you always. You can write a hex breaking incantation to wrap around the charm.

I haven't included a new botanical technique in this step. You've learned loads by now, so feel free to experiment with these two. Bay laurel can be burned in an abundance ritual, but it tends to crackle, and spark so be careful. You can crush pine cones and put a bit in your incense blends. If you have a fire pit, you can concentrate on your abundance intention while holding the cone and then toss it in the fire.

A terrific addition to these two is cinnamon. I love the slow burn of this botanical. Associated with prosperity, wealth and success. Also has a bit of a sexy side, so it can be very helpful if the abundance you seek is in the bedroom. Clover is my final recommendation: friendship, harmony, kindness, luck, money and wealth.

Stone

Green aventurine is the stone worked with in this step. Properties include: abundance, balance, creativity, clarity, creativity, independence, imagination, prosperity, protection, wealth and well-being. Cast a piece of aventurine when you need to decide about earthly possessions. You can draw a symbol for the object in the center of a piece of paper. Place "YES" on one side and "NO" on the other. Once you're attuned to the stone. Close your eyes, concentrate on your object and then drop the stone. Where it lands is guidance for your answer. Very simple divination technique.

You can make an abundance charm using the stone, bay leaves, and pine cones. Tie them all onto green cord. You can also add cinnamon sticks. Hang it by the main entrance to your home.

Other suitable stones:

- Citrine: wealth acquisition
- Tiger's Eye: prosperity. This is one of my favorites for prosperity magic. I've included a link in the Further Reading section to my popular prosperity spell.

Tarot

The sixes are about union, representing the last step before true unity. As you work on your magical life project, study the four sixes what are their messages for the life you are manifesting? The Lovers is a great card to contemplate about the meaning of abundance. Not just that way! They represent union, completion and wholeness.

The Bowl

Until this step, I've introduced one specific tool for in-depth study and use in each step. The emphasis of this step is very much on your choices. You choose what abundance means to you and craft a spell accordingly. I think you should also choose a tool that speaks the most to you for placement on your altar as a symbol of abundance. An offering bowl is the best symbol of abundance since by placing offerings to the energies, the worlds, the elements or deities and guides, we are acting from a position of abundance. We have plenty, so we share with others. Choose an offering bowl that appeals to you.

Make offerings to whatever energies you engage with and honor daily as part of your Witches' Hour of Power. They need not be complicated or time consuming. For example, since we are working with the element of earth in this step, you can choose offerings "of the earth" like leaves, dirt, etc. as appropriate for the deities that you honor.

The True Magic of Abundance

This step is all about the material world – things like health and wealth - and how to achieve your magical life. The balanced combination of Upper World (i.e., intellectual) energy with the purely Middle Self physical form (expressed through our emphasis on the element of earth) creates an atmosphere from which material matters can be explored without too much emotionality. Why is this the desired state? I'll put it like this: have you ever made a big-ticket purchase on impulse only to regret it later? When our attraction magic becomes too emotional, we can be at risk for that old shadow self to step forward.

REMINDER: the shadow is our companion and not to be dismissed. But, also not to be running our lives.

Attraction magic is usually best done from the opposite energetic perspective as removal witchery. Here in Step 6, you are at the other side of the transmutation work. Instead of changing thoughts and feelings from harmful to beneficial, you want to create purely beneficial ones. Don't forget that our actions need to be included in this recipe. I'll talk more about the Alignment of the Three Selves in this step which I refer to as "attunement."

The recipe for creating that magical life we all crave includes The Witches' Hour of Power, in this step the emphasis can be changed towards attraction magic by adding daily affirmations and gratitude practice. These are simple techniques that actualize the energy of true abundance. To put it simply, like attracts like.

I'm not saying that these practices are enough for manifesting your magical life. What I am claiming is that by shifting your energetic focus to emphasizing all that you already have, you'll open the energetic gateway for casting spells that will get you what you desire.

You've got all the skills needed to start working on your Magical Life Project. The idea of this grew from my personal project to create a life I love. It's been four years since I decided to radically change everything I was doing, from romantic relationships to finances. A lot got released to make the space for what I had started calling my Magical Life. As a family, we went through some awful times, including a horrible phase of not having any real home. It was chaotic, overwhelming and emotional. I'm blessed with two sons who trusted my every decision even when I wasn't entirely sure it was the right thing to do. Here we are in our dream home, in the perfect location, living a very magical life indeed. My days are spent exactly how I had always envisioned them. I have my ambitions and plans, but I'm pursuing them from a position of sovereignty. I am living an intentional life rather than an accidental one. I hope you find the project transformative. Know that it takes time. The creation of the vision is the first step. Keep at it and one day you'll wake up in your Magical Life as well.

Abundance, Gratitude and Prosperity

What is abundance? Is it being wealthy beyond our wildest dreams? Fame and fortune? I would argue that these things of themselves will never make us abundant. When they flow as a natural outcome of pursuing our Magical Life then they are born of the true self and not the shadow. Too many people focus on the financial side of things rather than the deeper processes that create an abundant state of being. I am using the terms "abundant" and "prosperous" interchangeably to refer to the state of having all that you truly need to get by. To me, "abundance" has always sounded like having too much. This is the mindset you want to adopt because this will give you excess to give away. Think of the Ace of Cups if you are into Tarot. An abundance mindset will render you like that overflowing cup.

If you are struggling with health problems, financial difficulties, problematic relationships, an unfulfilling career and other challenges, you may find it difficult to imagine a prosperous life. Abundance doesn't mean that all these issues completely disappear. What it does mean is that you engage in regular practices to remove the harmful energies brought on by these situations and to attract beneficial ones. This energetic shift completely works. The Magical Life Project will get you going on the right track.

The first leg of this journey is to start a daily abundance routine consisting of affirmations and gratitude practice. Why do this? Because it is flat-out impossible to create abundance if our energy if still primarily one of deficit. It's that simple. I am asking you to trust in the process of creating an abundance energy field. Six weeks of doing daily affirmation and gratitude practice will render amazing results.

Affirmation Magic

Affirmations, like abundance, are very personal. The basic technique is to write affirmative statements using "I" about your abilities, attributes and skills. The focus should be on your characteristics rather than achievements. Appearance can sometimes be included in this practice if the statement reflects your own abilities or accomplishments rather than any type of comparison. Affirmations should be about sustainable things rather than fleeting ones. Affirmations are primarily Upper Self energy, although they have emotional consequences. Record your affirmations in your journal with an explanation of why you want to emphasize that construct. Do your affirmations work first thing in the morning.

Daily Gratitude Ritual

Gratitude is of the Lower Self since it is primarily emotional. Since we are focusing on the attunement of the Three Selves, choose one thing that represents each one. This helps us to see the interconnectedness between the Three Selves. For example, "I am grateful for the considerate way the cashier treated me," is an emotional statement while "I am grateful that traffic was easy on the way home" is much more Middle Self because it refers to an action. Expressing gratitude for helpful advice or learning from a book are examples of Upper World energy. Play around with your gratitude statements. Explore how each one evokes a different feeling inside of you. As with the affirmations, use your "I" statements. Unlike affirmations which are about fixed constructs, gratitude is about transient things. Of course, they can both be the opposite, too. As you are developing your practices, try to keep this distinction. It will help create sustained abundance energy (affirmations) and in-the-moment as well (gratitude).

The daily gratitude practice that I'm suggesting is a simple ritual done in the evening, usually before bedtime. Use three candles of your choosing and write three gratitude statements in your journal. Then recite each statement as you light a candle. After the candles are lit, focus on the feeling of gratitude inside you. Envision it spreading out to the candles, infusing them with the feeling of being completely blessed. Some days you'll feel like there is an abundance of this energy. When this happens send it to those you are grateful for.

The Power of Offerings
Being grateful to the elements and the Three Worlds for their energy
through offerings using the bowl on the altar
Attracts abundance
From them.

When we make offerings to the energies, guides, deities or ancestors that we work with and honor, we are expressing something beyond gratitude. To me, these actions are a combination of affirmations and gratitude since these things exist within and without. Some people honor deities as a way of keeping away "bad" energy. This is not my personal practice. I stay away from that mindset entirely. I am grateful always for the blessings I have received.

A great example of an offering for this step would be a small live plant placed on the altar. Offerings can also be acts of service. For example, when doing Under World healing, you can pick up litter from a beach. Magic fires can be lit as an offering for the combination of the seven, with a ritual of gratitude for each element of fire. Water to put out the flames is the last one.

A simple daily offering of thanks can be added to your specific gratitude ritual. "To the Element of Earth, I bless you through my offering of taking care of this plant" or "To the Upper World, I bless you through this offering of the purified air created by this plant." You get the idea. Plants can be used as offerings for all the seven energies since they include all of them. Develop your own ritual using a plant or fire. Do this practice after your daily gratitude ritual. You'll see amazing results in a few short weeks.

Attracting Abundance
Now that you are establishing your daily abundance practices, you'll start to see the shift in your mindset and energy field. Ensure that you are observing everything that is happening

to you during this transition. Better things will automatically start to come your way. When you add intentional magic like with our Magical Life project, the results are amplified. Make sure you journal through this transition, so you can track the changes. Affirmations, gratitude and offerings make us aware of all that we already possess. Once this practice is established, you'll obtain clarity in what you need to manifest abundance as you define it. There are several types of attraction magic: abundance, prosperity, healing, divination, etc.

Abundance is generally the goal of attraction magic. We rarely seek to manifest just enough to get by. Prosperity is our goal, whether in health, work, relationship, financial or other matters. We can combine removal aspects in our magic by using a complex blend of correspondences. In this step, I've presented ones that are used purely as attractors. When you write your own spells, consider the interactions between correspondences that are of different polarities (i.e., attraction v. removal). This makes for a much more complex spell, but when properly done yields amazing results.

Abundance and Color Magic

Color magic is based on the energetic properties of a certain shade. The composition of the molecules, including pigments, causes light to refract in separate ways leading to our perception of a specific color. If that isn't True Magic then I don't know what is. Green is obviously the color many of us associate with abundance. It's the color of the bounty found in the summer. Of course, it's also the color of money. But, there are other colors we can associate with our definition of prosperity. The standard energies of the colors are great, but there are also the personal ones. I had this dream of owning a grey SUV, so for me, abundance was associated with this color. When I finally purchased a brand new one, I felt very prosperous. We've worked with the energy of the colors throughout this book. When crafting your Magical

Life project that you'll learn about in the next few pages, review how the colors of True Magic have been used so far and add your own shades of significance.

The traditional witches' colors are black, white and red. Black is for the Lower Self/Under World, red is for the Middle Self and World and white is for the Higher Self and Upper World. The combination of the three yields purple, our sovereign self. When we add the elements, red is also applied to fire, blue is for water, yellow for air and green for earth. You can find more in *Llewellyn's Book of Correspondences* or Buckland's classic *Color Magic*. Since affirmations are a focus of this step, I've included one for each color as examples to inspire you when creating your own set.

Black as night,
Red as blood,
White as stars.

Colors can be woven into an incantation, like the classic lines above. For representations of the colors used in a working, candles are the most common choice followed by crystals. Use inks and paper in appropriate shades as well. And don't forget to weave color magic into your appearance and home.

Energetic Properties of Colors

Here's a list of the energetic properties of colors that you can use in all sorts of True Magic, including crafting your Magical Life Project, including the Vision Board and the ensuing spell.

Black: Banishing; mediumship; protection (sending away); reversal
White: Psychic development; protection (attracting); purification
Red: Creativity; passion; romance; sexuality

Orange: Career; children; education; relationships
Yellow: Assertiveness; confidence; self-esteem
Pink: Compassion; happiness; kindness; love
Green: Attracting objects and possessions; abundance; finances; money; major purchases; property
Blue: Training; talking; teaching; thoughts; writing
Purple: Self-control; connection to the deities and other entities; integrity; Other World workings; sovereignty
Brown: Add to Middle World workings; spells about the land and property
Silver: Use as a symbol of the unified self
Gold: All the elements and the Three Worlds combined

Planetary Magic and Abundance

I wanted to talk a bit about planetary magic and how you can weave it throughout your Magical Life Project. The Seven Wandering Stars have been used for True Magic throughout history. The two more recently discovered planets can also be used in magic, though I only use the seven original ones that are at times visible in the night sky. As I'm writing this, Mars is the closest to the Earth that's it's been in decades. I've been doing magic for courage using the energy of the red planet.

Working with astrological correspondences is typically viewed as high magic since it is not only associated with the Upper World but also the power of the mind. Like colors, planets have archetypes. Unlike those of colors – we all know red is associated with fire, blue with water and so on – we may not already have a sense or knowledge about the planets, moon and sun. Like Words of Power, the origins of planetary magic stretch back through time and across cultures.

The way we connect with these celestial objects is through their archetypes. These are the dominant energy signatures of the moon, sun and five visible planets. Each one has a different archetype that is found across traditions and systems. Venus, you probably already know, is associated with love and romance. Mercury is all about trickery and communication. Who hasn't heard of the chaos that ensues when this planet appears to go backwards? Mars is the planet to connect with when you need to go into battle, while Saturn will help reveal the metaphysical worlds to us. Jupiter is a planet for sovereignty magic. The moon has many characteristics in modern witchcraft, especially for magic and divination. The fiery energy of the sun reflects growth, action and prophecy.

The ways we can harness planetary energies include: evocation, direction and connection. Planetary energies can be added to spells by concentrating on the archetype while crafting the symbol into an incantation or sigil. Mercury is a good one to add to any sort of working where communication is vital or when you need a swift result. Mercury energy needs to be directed, so ensure that you summon it accordingly. Apply the same techniques to planetary connections as you do for botanical or stone spirit magic. Use the list below to activate your Magical Life Project. Include their symbols in your Vision Board, spell and other types of witchery.

The Energetic Characteristics of the Seven Wandering Stars

Include the symbols of corresponding planets in all your spells, sigils and other workings. They really boost the energy. Connect to planetary energies by studying images of the planets. Drawing down the energy of a planet is the same as harnessing the moon's power, so use the technique outlined for lunar energy use earlier in this book.

Witch Tip: Using the colors + the planets to create symbols and sigils is one of my most preferred techniques. Double magic.

Sun: Healing, energy, pride, dignity, self-expression,

individuality. Symbol: circle. Yellow.

Moon: Emotions, rebirth, self-discovery, revelations, divination. Circle with a dot in the middle. See earlier discussion for colors of the phases, the general color for moon magic is white.

Mercury: Communication, intellect, curiosity, business, commerce, education, divination. Stick figure with small horns. Blue.

Venus: Desire, love, friendship, creativity, sensuality, sexuality, romance, relationships, affection. Stick figure. Green.

Mars: Aggression, courage, disciplined action, self-motivation, impulsivity, success in conflict, retribution. The male symbol, circle with a line pointing northeast with an arrow at the end. Red.

Jupiter: Healing, compassion, idealism, sovereignty, charity. The symbol looks like a fancy four. Purple.

Saturn: Judgment, rules, restrictions, fate, responsibilities, determination, justice, cursing. A fancy small "h" is the symbol. Black.

Affirmations Using Color Magic and Planetary Energies

Here are seven examples harnessing the planetary energies into affirmations, along with the color correspondence. Use these as part of your practice or (better yet) inspiration when creating your own affirmations. Wear the colors associated with each one to add oomph to your affirmation for the day. Write each intention with the corresponding planetary symbol on pieces of paper and carry with you to activate the power of the affirmation. Try one each day for a week, recording your results.

Encouraging self-discipline: The principle is "to be silent." Connect with Venus and green. *I have excellent self-control.*

Increasing awareness: To know, increased by the yellow

energy of the sun. *I am aware of all things that serve my truth.*

Maximizing strength: To will, red and Mars will help you achieve this. *My will is strong, and my intention true.*

Activating sovereignty: To dare, blue and Mercury instill greater freedom. *I claim my sovereignty.*

Power boost: To go, the purple power surge of Jupiter will increase. *I draw all my power back to me.*

Confidence top up: To feel, Saturn and black energize your self-esteem. *I am proud of my abilities.*

Integrity increase: To believe, the pureness of white and the moon strengthen character. *I honor my ways and words.*

What is a Magical Life?

- The true self shines and the shadow is tamed
- Abundance and prosperity as you define them
- Using all your innate abilities and learned skills to your highest good
- Being connected to all three selves, both their form and force
- Manifesting all that you need to thrive
- Connecting to the seven energetic forces
- Having an intentional, curious and passionate approach to life
- Being kind (not nice...that's fake, I'm talking about compassion)
- Having the material possessions, you desire
- Financial stability
- Good health
- Positive relationships
- Having interests, hobbies and activities that you love doing
- Experiencing a full range of emotions
- Ruling your thoughts rather than them running the show
- Honoring your physical body through activities and

practices (like healthy eating, giving up addictions)
- A fulfilling career
- A secure home and property

I'm sure that I've missed things that are part of your personal definition of a Magical Life. That's why it's so important to take the time to contemplate how you define abundance. Begin this project by making a list of the ingredients of your Magical Life.

The Magical Life Journey

This is a Visionary Revelations journey. Perhaps you already have an idea of what your Magical Life will be like, but maybe not. This journey will help you to clarify or reveal what your magical life will be. I do this sort of journey in the bath, so I can be as open as possible. It can also be done lying down. Being as relaxed as possible is necessary for this journey. Most of our journey work so far has involved travelling outward, especially to the Other World. In this one, we go deep inside to reveal what we already know: what our true self wants to manifest.

I'm adding a caveat here before we get into discussing the details – the witches' journey is epic not easy. Creating your Magical Life may require great transformation and what seems like sacrifice at the time. In addition, we have all gone through periods of suffering. Creating a magic life doesn't mean that there will be no more pain. It means that you have all the skills available to make the most of it. To turn trash into treasure, if you will. That is True Magic.

For the journey, you can incorporate the aventurine using one of the methods presented in an earlier step. Arrange the bay leaf and pine cone blend on a fire proof plate. You can add a layer of sea salt underneath for a nice boost. Cinnamon can also be added. That way you can light the bay if you wish. It will only burn for a brief time. You can burn the green candle for this step if you wish. This will create a calm energy of abundance, while both the bay and pine will help open your inner gates.

Extinguish both before beginning your journey to be safe. Standard ritual procedures should be followed. Doing this at the start of the waxing moon will ensure that you are ready for spell casting at its height.

The focus of this journey is to reveal *your ideal day* this will provide the framework for the rest of the activities of the Magical Life Project. When we know what our perfect day looks like, we can start to manifest it.

When you are ready, get comfortable. Make sure that you are warm.

If you are wound up, start with The True Magic Meditation to balance your energies.

Begin by focusing on your breath. Breathe in fully and slowly filling your lungs, belly, drawing it all the way down to your toes. Exhale slowly, releasing the transformed breath into what is needed by the material world. The plants give us air and we return it. This is natural abundance being exchanged.

Turn your attention to your third eye. It activates. Opening into your innermost being. The core truth of the Three Selves, your soul. You may experience these energies as pure black, red and white cords running throughout your physical being, all tension and pretense is washed away, leaving only the purest truth. Slowly the cords start to form into a vision. It is you waking up. Take note of your immediate surroundings. Who, if anyone, is with you? What time is it? What are you wearing?

You gently get out of bed to start the day. Notice your activities as you get ready for the day ahead, what you wear, eat, where you go and do. Remain the detached observer. Remember that this is a vision quest of revelation. Let the day's events flow like a movie. Take note of everything that is revealed as you make your way through the morning, lunch, afternoon, supper and the evening. If anything is unclear, travel back in time over the events of the day until you have a complete vision of what your ideal day is.

When you are ready, let the black, red and white cords cover the vision gently. Slowly close your internal third eye. Bring yourself back into the present through calming breaths. Wiggle your toes and fingers. Lay there while you review the vision. When ready, write about your experience.

Magical Life Vision Board

Now that you've received the vision of your ideal day, it's time to expand it. A Vision Board is a wonderful manifesting tool. Creating a board brings into clear focus what your magical life looks like. You can use photos, quotes, images, etc. For the board, you can purchase an inexpensive cork board or use a stiff sheet of art board. I don't recommend thin poster board because it tends to curl. You want your board to last. A new way to design a vision board is on your computer or device. I've included the new one I made as part of writing this step in the Photo Gallery. Apps that I love are Fotor, Canva, WordArt and PowerPoint. If you're new to digital witchery, there are loads of tutorials that you can watch on YouTube.

I have my Vision Board as the wallpaper on my devices. I printed a copy that hangs right beside my desk. If you can't display it in your personal space, having it on your device ensures that you'll be able to connect to it at least once a day.

Start by selecting a time frame for this vision board. The one I did while developing this step was for two years, but I've done them for six months and one year as well. Choose a timeframe that works for you. You want to build in success, so keep it about material aspects of your Magical Life.

Identifying Themes

Write the key points of from your Ideal Day Vision Quest on cue cards or construction paper, using markers/crayons that correspond to the colors we use or use the chakra colors if they appeal to you, or even both. You can also do this on your device. I still do this part on paper because I find that creating tangible things at the initial stages of any project very helpful for achieving focus.

Choosing Images

Once you've identified your themes, select images to go with each one. I also make text boxes of specific goals and include corresponding quotes. The planetary symbols are an excellent addition. Place them next to corresponding goals.

Infusing the Board with Intention

As you create the board, infuse each image or word with energy. You can internally chant, "I am manifesting my magical life. I do so by claiming _____." Fill in the blank for the specific intention, such as a new job, improved relationship, living a healthy lifestyle, etc. Use color and planetary energy to boost each intention. Follow this by writing down the specific steps that will manifest each part of your vision board. Chose goals that you can successfully manifest with all that is available to you. These will form the basis for your magical life spell.

Keep your Vision Board in your magic space if it is near your bed, if not, make a space just for the Vision Board near your bed or wherever you consider your private space. That way you can meditate using the Board as a focus each morning and evening.

Your Magical Life Spell

This spell is entirely of your own design. The one thing I'll mention is that this should be done during the waxing moon. Go back through this book for all the various parts of True Magic spell development you've learned: intention writing, incantation development, choosing correspondences, creating magic space, evoking the energies, and more.

Ending This Step

End this step with the green candle following the same ritual you've done at the end of each step. Refresh the offerings to the elements and worlds in your bowl. If you haven't used the aventurine in a charm or the spell, you can add it to your altar as well. Save your daily gratitude work to be done during this Step Completion Ceremony. After you light the candle do these practices, then focus on the positive energy you've created reverberating up and out. Then see it all coming back down to you many times over. All energy grows, so shall your abundance.

Further Reading

Blogs

Mat Auryn, *The Magick of Affirmations.* Available at: http://www.patheos.com/blogs/matauryn/2018/01/01/affirmations/

Cyndi Brannen, *Prosperity Magick: A Spell and Correspondences.* Available at: http://www.patheos.com/blogs/keepingherkeys/2018/03/crafting-a-prosperity-potion/

Books

Michael Bernard Beckwith, *Life Visioning: A Transformative Process for Activating Your Unique Gifts and Highest Potential*

Raymond Buckland, *Practical Color Magick*

Denning and Phillips, *Planetary Magick*

Lisa Nichols, *Abundance Now*

Wholeness

Wholeness is an ongoing process that occurs within all areas of ourselves and the external energies. It is about harmony within ourselves, our immediate surroundings, our homes but also our workplaces. The place to begin to experience the flow of unity is within ourselves. Ownership is the pursuit of wholeness. This refers to being in control of all that we are and possess. How many times have you heard – or said yourself – "own it"?

Starting this Step

Begin this step is by taking some time to review everything that you've accomplished to this point. When I am doing this sort of contemplation magic, I often set up an altar with the key correspondences, symbols and tools of the part of my journey that I am thinking about. Sometimes these are the botanicals, stones and tools that we have a natural affinity with. More often, in my experience, it's the ones that gave me trouble when I first started using them that I end up being closest to. Resistance shows itself in many forms, including the things we use to make magic. Of course, there are those things to which I simply can't relate. Only through exploring these items can we determine if it's resistance or disparity that is blocking our connection.

Reviewing our journals is an excellent means of evaluating progress, yet another reason why it is so vital to keep great records. Look back at what you were writing about at the beginning of your journey with True Magic. Go a step further to look at the structure of your writing. Do you use more "I" statements now? Is your magic more action oriented and about solving problems? I bet you can see the shift from an accidental life to an intentional since you began. Your Inner Witch is standing proud.

At the end of this step, you can do a self-initiation ritual to recognize your achievement of unleashing your Inner Witch. As you conduct your review and construct a contemplative altar, you can start to think about this ritual.

The self-initiation should be completed during the Full Moon, so plan your magic for this step accordingly. The Starry Road Rebirth Journey is best done during the days just before the Full Moon. I don't recommend doing both workings together. You could do the Starry Road one evening and then the initiation the next.

Full Moon

The full moon embodies wholeness. It is the time when the suns' energy reflects the greatest on its surface, shining down the on the earth. The full moon also has the greatest impact on the tides. It is the period when the Three Worlds aspects of the moon are most apparent. The moon itself is a mediator between the earth and sun, but also has a unique influence on the earth. The full moon is a gateway to Upper World work.

The Energy of the Upper World

The journey is almost complete. We've travelled from the depths of the Under World and the Lower Self through the Middle World to arrive here in the upper reaches of our human understanding. The air here is refined and light. Too much time in the Upper World can leave us feeling disconnected. This is reflected in our everyday lives when we are too "up in our head."

Divination using Tarot cards can be situated as Upper World magic since we use the visual images with our intuitive thoughts and standard definitions to interpret the messages of individual cards and in a spread. The energy is primarily intellectual, though our reactions can be very emotional. Contrast this to the early steps where the dominant energy was emotional followed by thoughts and the balanced action-oriented steps on growth, connection and abundance. Here in the Upper World, we turn our gaze to the Starry Road above and our Higher Selves.

While I was writing this step, I kept thinking about the Higher Self in its purest form. The pure intellect. The sort of ideal that philosophers have been writing about for centuries. I would contend that our eternal soul is not merely this, but also includes the eternal parts of the Lower and Middle Selves. These are our Three Souls. We also have our Three Shadows. The shadows are part of the selves and souls. All combine into wholes – the self, the soul and the shadow. As humans, we can journey to the rarified air of the Upper World, the domain of angels, stars and the moon, but we don't belong there for too long. The climate is not suited for us. It is an appropriate place to travel for a mystical rebirth journey since the conditions will strip us clean to the bones and build us back up from our internal star dust. Truth will be revealed, and wholeness will be that much closer under the brilliant light of the full moon.

Correspondences

Wholeness is associated with the color **white**, shamanism and rebirth. The butterfly is also associated with unity, transformation and rebirth. Butterfly energy would be a powerful addition to the content of this step if you are interested. The color white is also associated with psychic activation (white star energy found on The Starry Road), beginnings (you'll be reborn), change (obvious), clarity, focus, enlightenment (the stuff of the Higher Self), higher power, protection and visions. Consider wearing white for the Starry Road journey. For the self-initiation ceremony, you should wear black.

The number **seven** is associated with white, moonstone, the clair's (clairaudience, clairvoyance, clairsentience, etc.), completion, rebirth, the mind, and the Upper World.

White and seven are also symbolic of the crown chakra, physically located at the top of the head. This is "beyond the third eye" to the place of higher consciousness, where we can perceive unity within and without. The crown chakra links us to higher consciousness and enlightenment. It is the portal to the Upper World. The portion of this we visit is called The Starry Road.

Botanicals

Elm is associated with beginnings, rebirth, grace, intuition, stability, compassion, grace and wisdom. The card of elm is the Wheel of Fortune. You can use elm in a variety of forms, from powdered slippery to fresh leaves. Slippery elm as a tonic will support your Upper World work in this step. About ¼ tsp. per cup of boiled water. Adjust to taste.

Elm leaves can be placed on your altar to help you through the rebirth process. In whatever form you choose, keep elm close during this step, especially the Starry Road journey. For the more experienced consumer of botanicals, mugwort can be added to the slippery elm tonic.

Myrrh comes along to open us up to our Higher Selves and higher consciousness. While elm supports our Starry Road magic, myrrh paves the way. I love working with this resin, but when I am not actively engaged with it I must keep it tightly sealed and in a locked cupboard because I am super sensitive to its abilities. Myrrh can be used in its natural resin or as an oil. I always use it as a resin, burning it as part of a mixed incense. If I burn it on its own, I end up getting too far up in the air. Terrible headaches ensue, so use myrrh wisely. If you have access to sandalwood that can be substituted or Palo Santo.

Myrrh's properties are an excellent addition to all sorts of psychic workings, especially for death-rebirth magic. It is also a potent psychic ability activator. A quirky side of myrrh is that it is a powerful addition to abundance spells. You can purchase it already ground or do it yourself in a mortar and pestle. Place a small amount (think baby finger nail sized) on a slightly larger piece of charcoal. It's great for charging the cards when you want a strong reading, for aiding plant spirit connection, etc. I find it is also great for facilitating spirit communication, especially the Upper World kind or some departed humans. Depends on their personality.

To help with your journey, you can grind about 1 tsp. of elm with a chunk of myrrh resin and then mix with moonstone chips to make a potent conduit to the Starry Road. Place this beside you on your journey. There's no need to burn it to activate the properties, just leave it in an open dish.

Additional botanicals include marjoram and rose. You can substitute sage for myrrh, although it is nowhere near the Upper World specialist that myrrh is.

Stone

Moonstone, one of my favorites, is the stone for this step. It is an excellent stone to use as a connector when contacting spirits, such as meeting your new guide in the Starry Road Journey. Other properties of moonstone include: clairvoyance, psychic ability, and wisdom. This diverse stone can be used for a variety of purposes ranging from accomplishments, agriculture, emotions, enchantment, happiness, sleep and youth. Perhaps most relevant to this step is that is facilitates unity of the Three Selves. Like the moon itself, it is a stone that includes the Three Worlds. It is Upper World in its properties for psychic ability, Lower World for magic and emotions, and Middle World for its use for very practical matters and deeds.

A chunk of moonstone placed at the crown of your head during the journey in this step will help ensure your Upper World connection. You can also use moonstone chips in a variety of ways. If you have long hair, they can be woven into a braid or bun. Make a seven-pointed moonstone charm by pressing it into polymer clay. Keep your moonstone with a chunk of myrrh to render it more attuned to psychic visions. Remember that stones with diverse properties like moonstone can benefit from this sort of attunement to better enhance your use of it during focused workings. I like placing the chips on body meridians to help with astral travel and other Upper World witcheries.

Additional stones can include ones suited for mysticism, such as a clear quartz point. Fluorite has always performed well for me as an Upper World stone. Blue agate can be added to facilitate communication with your new spirit guide.

Tarot

The Chariot, Judgment (in some decks this is Rebirth), Death, The Star and The World are all suitable cards to study to help you better understand the process of rebirth into your magical life and the pursuit of unity.

The Censer

The censer is the tool for this step. Censers are vessels containing incense that is burned or heated to release their properties into the air. There is something so primal about burning myrrh in a censer. The smoke alters the chemical structure of the air it touches, rendering the entire space into a portal to what lies beyond. It's a gateway to the Upper World, death and rebirth. Proceed with caution. Heed my suggestion for burning about a finger nail sized chunk of ground myrrh. If using essential oil, then the diffuser is the censer. A censer certainly can be electric. Any heat-proof bowl can be used for the censer. If you can't burn or heat the essential oils, placing the botanicals on a special dish without altering them can be used as a substitution.

The censer is a tool of smoke, so it is most associated with the Upper World and the element of air.

Censers hold a place of importance in most religions and paths around the world. The ceremonial burning of incense is a vital part of rituals across cultures. I burn something almost every day as part of my Witches' Hour of Power.

Understanding Wholeness

Wholeness as a construct is something that gets tossed around a lot in modern spirituality. The basic idea is usually "we are one with the universe and each other." This is a lofty ideal, but it is sound and applies to the type of unity we seek in witchery. My issue with this approach is that the emphasis is too much on connecting to others and the universe rather than unifying our own selves. As witches we know "as within, so without." Attunement to the energy of others and the even energies in their external forms will never happen unless we do so within ourselves.

Wholeness is an ongoing process that occurs within all areas of ourselves and the external energies. It is about harmony within ourselves, our immediate surroundings, our homes but also our workplaces. The place to begin to experience the flow of unity is within ourselves. Ownership is what I call being in pursuit of wholeness within. This refers to being in control of all that we are and possess

Initiation is a form of rebirth. In the self-initiation process, you'll experience a powerful ritual and create your own talisman and cingulum to mark the wholeness of unifying your Inner Witch with the external forces.

I mentioned in the last unit that abundance flows towards us best when our Upper World aspects are more dominant in our decision-making process. This isn't a denial of our other two selves, but permits their energies be filtered through our intellect, including the power of thought. I talk a bit about how to maximize your thoughts in this step in the concepts section.

Symbol

The Septagram represents wholeness among the seven external energies and reflects your achievement of all the steps in this book. It is also the symbol of the Upper World. This symbol, like I wrote way back in the introduction is found in various forms across different paths throughout recorded history. You can also see it as The Selves and Worlds each representing one point with the seventh being "ether" – all that is beyond. This is like the way that the pentagram is often interpreted, with the four elements and the fifth being "everything else."

The septagram is the star, that bright light in the night sky. It is symbolic of the Upper World, astrological magic, alchemy, psychic visions and other types of what is commonly called "high magic". This star reflects the state of unity that we pursue as we create our magical life. It is to this star that you'll travel to during the rebirth journey in this step.

Wholeness and Consciousness

Wholeness includes our conscious experience and all that lies in the subconscious. The awakened, unleashed witch travels to the heights of consciousness to understand and challenge its boundaries. Consciousness is like its Upper World botanical product, smoke. Like smoke, it is something that is easy to perceive but challenging to explain. Neither exist without something – another force – making them. Our consciousness is the energetic container for our intellect, thoughts and gateway to the mysteries. I've been fascinated by consciousness since grad school when I did a huge project (known as a Comprehensive, appropriately titled) on different perspectives on the self. That we can hold ourselves to be the object of study, including our own thoughts, is known as metacognition. Thinking about thinking. In terms of mundane human experiences, this is the closest we can get to our mystical Higher Self.

Aligning the Three Selves

Connecting to our Higher Self is the final step of releasing our Inner Witch. As witches, we actively seek experiences beyond the mundane. Most people remain in the lower areas of the Higher Self. I am advocating for pushing our experience of consciousness further, beyond trance. This type of exploration is very demanding. It requires a process of death and rebirth into a unified being. To do this type of work, we need to first align the Three Selves as much as possible. I've been writing about attunement of The Three Selves for the past few steps. By now, you should be feeling internally harmonious. This is the state of flow – effortless and unselfconscious sovereignty. That is the experience of attunement. Your thoughts, actions and feelings are all working together. Your three souls are subsequently more accessible. This includes the part of our Higher Self that is the eternal intellect.

The Higher Self is the gateway to expanded consciousness, to being able to perceive unity in all things. By turning our energetic gaze upward, we become aware of the connections within and without, above and below. This state is beyond attunement of the selves. The Higher Self includes our thoughts but travels further upward to what is commonly known as our crown chakra. The fact that awareness and interest in the Higher Self has so greatly increased in recent decades is a sign that humanity is transitioning. The Higher Self can express what is known by the Three Souls (our eternal parts) in a way that we can understand. Often, the Higher Self breaks through into our everyday consciousness as intuition. We experience the lower reaches of the Higher Self through our intellectual abilities.

Seven Aspects of Intellect

Our intellect is a mighty tool. A lot of times we think about intellect in relation to structured learning or reading "intellectual" books. Intellect is not limited to these activities. In our daily lives, we use our intellect to process our thoughts, actions and emotions.

Nonjudgment refers to the active attempt at trying not to be judgmental. Being a whole witch gives you the power to pause before jumping to conclusions. *Patience* is practiced through acceptance. It is learning *emotional courage* to handle distressing feelings well. You began your journey of unleashing with a *beginner's mind* - motivated to understand more about ourselves and witchcraft. *Leaning in* is about refusing to be resistant. It is about having a growth mindset rather than a fixed one, not that we are lazy. Striving implies fighting against unmanageable forces. Sovereignty teaches us that we are powerful. The fight becomes winnable. *Letting go* is what we do to the shadow as we move through the steps, especially in our healing. *Wholeness* is the end result of all the other aspects.

Journal Prompt: Do an inventory of each one of these aspects in your journal over the course of a week.

Ownership

Ownership is how we express our sovereign power. Ownership is a mindset wherein the Three Selves are attuned, our connection to the upper reaches of the Higher Self is established and we live as our True Self. This is unity in action. From here, we begin to create our magical lives. Our witchery becomes much more powerful as well. How do we practice ownership? Not surprisingly, it is in everything we feel, do and think. Below is a simple technique to help you understand how to better "own" your thoughts.

Unity

In magic, unity refers to the synergistical attunement of all the parts. It's another word for wholeness. Without unifying intention, incantation, correspondences, objects, magic spaces and ourselves to the task at hand, all we've got are a bunch of cool things and a promising idea. Magic is the unification process. Creating a magical life is the same. We seek unity. Perfect love and perfect trust. As above, so below. As within, so without. *So speak I and it is true.* You've been practicing unity each time you've done The True Magic Meditation.

Unity is truth, truth is magic. Separation, discord, is an illusion.
It is the work of the shadow telling us that magic isn't real.
That we can't have a magical life. Magical thinking is the active
belief that unity is possible. Creativity is how we express the
development of unity.

There is a time for separation, the need for it is protective:
"I need to detach." Unplug. When we are attuned, the need for
separation is a conscious choice. When we aren't, we live our
lives in separation. Awareness of the separation and the ensuing
desire for wholeness is a sure sign that your Inner Witch is fully
empowered. All spiritual paths are about the quest for unity.
Kabbalistic concept of oneness, Einstein's Unified Field Theory,
yoga, New Age Thought. Unity seems to be the goal of most
religions and spiritual paths, but what does this mean for us
witches? The Witches' Journey is to the quest for the wholeness
of unity.

The chant below can be added to your Witches' Hour of
Power to encourage and strengthen your internal unity.

May I be healing.
May I be accepting.
May I be sovereign.
May I be growing.
May I be connected.
May I be abundant.
May I be whole.

Spiritual Alchemy

Wholeness is an ongoing process, I liken it to spiritual alchemy
where the seven principles are continually broken down,
cleansed and then unified into a synergistic product that we call
unity. Wholeness through dissolution and rebuilding is what we
do in True Magic. Using the alchemical process as a metaphor
for our internal unification process can help us better understand

the transformation we have achieved. Although there are no standard seven steps in alchemy, the process can be divided into these stages: calcination, dissolution, separation, conjunction, fermentation, distillation and fermentation.

Calcination

In this step, the substance is heated over a flame until it is reduced to ashes. The healing process is much like this. We use fire to burn away all that causes us pain.

Dissolution

The next stage is to dissolve the ashes into water. Thus, beginning the process of transformation. The ashes represent the beginning of our understanding of energy. They are also symbolic of the process of transmutation; changing the original state of an object (feelings, thoughts, actions) into the opposite. You can liken dissolution as the process of creating healthy boundaries where the ashes of our pain are poured into the essence of our being to help create positive relationships.

Separation

In separation, the products of dissolution are isolated and filtered. We crafted a concentrated oil by dissolving the botanicals into their individual properties and then bringing them back together. The oil activated our sovereignty which itself is a process of separating from enmeshment with others.

Conjunction

In Step 4, the focus was on understanding the energy of the Middle Self and to activate growth. This is comparable to the alchemical stage of conjunction where a new substance is formed from the separated elements that we choose to keep. After the first three steps, your chosen focus for growth emerged from the ashes of the stripping away process.

Fermentation

This is the step of breaking down a substance with bacteria or other micro-organisms. Consider the process of making wine. The grapes need to rot to release the properties necessary to create something wonderful. In Step 5, the process moved further into creation by exploring our connections to all things.

Distillation

This is the process of boiling a solution and condensing it to achieve purity. When we consider what prosperity and abundance means to us, there is a necessary process of distilling that occurs. We asked ourselves, "what does prosperity mean to me?" This stripping down can lead to a "pure" pursuit of our magical life.

Coagulation

The final alchemical process that I'm including is coagulation; the transformation of the liquid into a solid state. All the ingredients become unified into a new creation. This reflects the current exploration of unity and rebirth into our magical life. After the ritual (and self-initiation if you choose to do it), you are coagulated – or reborn – as a new you that consists of all the best parts of yourself with that which doesn't serve you burned and boiled away. Purity, not perfection, is the result. We are our true selves – or Materia Prima.

This model of spiritual alchemy is like shamanic perspectives which we use throughout the course. The rebirth journey you'll soon be doing is directly based on my training in shamanic style dismemberment and death journeying.

Spiritual Alchemy of Botanicals

Spagyrics is alchemy involving botanicals. This exercise explores plant consciousness using this alchemical perspective.

Botanicals and stones, like all other entities, present in

different ways based on our traits, needs, experiences and their psycho-spiritual properties. Botanicals and stones can be conduits through which "greater" entities, like deities, speak. There are, I believe, energetic currents that provide guidance along our path. This can be understood by many names. They connect to us through our Higher Selves which, although separate from our Middle Self is very much connected to our lived experience and abilities. How we perceive their energies is influenced by our psychic abilities. These include the "clairs," such as clairvoyance, clairaudience and clairsentience.

You've completed several different plant spirit connection exercises by now. One final technique that I wanted to share with you uses a spagyrical approach. To understand the wholeness of a botanical, we can further understand a plant as consisting of salt, sulfur and mercury. These are the three basic alchemical concepts. Sulphur is the soul, mercury is the life force and salt is the physical body.

To understand botanical consciousness better, use this approach to connect to a living plant. If possible, use one of the recommended botanicals for this step. Interpret the following based on the communication from the plant. What is the sulphur of the plant? The mercury? The salt? How do these aspects unify the plant? Then divide the known properties and correspondences of the botanical into these three categories. For example, the "sulphur" of mugwort would be magic. The mercury would be properties such as "psychic aid" and "protection." The salt would be its physical appearance and known correspondences, like "green" and the elements of air and earth. You can include the planetary correspondences, days of the week, numbers, Tarot cards and deities. These are all physical representations or the salt of the plant. Explore the unified description you have created using this approach.

Record this technique in your BoS and begin to apply it to the other plants, stones and correspondences you use.

This alchemical approach is another way we can hone our understanding of wholeness and how we can use them in our witchery. The more we understand wholeness and pursue unity in our spells, the more effective they become.

The Meaning of Spiritual Death and Rebirth

In alchemy there is the necessary process of breaking down the parts of a substance in order to rearrange them into a pure product. Being spiritually dead occurs when the shadow self is in control. The symptoms include: feeling stuck, elevated levels of distress, poor decision making, addictions, personal crises and ineffective magic. Typically, our emotions are numbed or inappropriate during spiritual death. Our energy goes into resistance, fear and other destructive processes. We are the opposite of whole. The steps in this book have supported you while you released your Inner Witch. Standing here now, in your true self, you can feel the shimmer of wholeness on your skin and in your heart. The last step on this awakening process is to let die all that no longer serves you. This is intentional spiritual death rather than the automatic kind that results when we are living a false life.

Does killing these parts of ourselves damage our shadow? No. The shadow is part of who we are. What the spiritual death process does is remove burdens from it. The past is released. The pain inflicted by others, the lies we've told ourselves and the accumulated feelings of isolation are dissolved. The shadow is healed.

The shamanic practice of disintegration provides a framework for understanding this process. In this model, all that doesn't serve us is "killed" and we are dissolved down to our essence. In alchemical terms this is the remaining ash. This is the essence of our spirit, our Three Souls. Through rebirth, we are built from this ash anew. Coagulated into our true selves, unified within. From this position, we can pursue unity and create our magical lives.

Starry Road Rebirth Journey

This rebirth journey takes place in the Upper World, along The Starry Road. The Starry Road is the energetic entrance to the mystical Upper World. In some traditions, this is the "road of spirits." It is to here that we travel to meet our guide that will see us through the rebirth process. As we travel down the road, the guide will reveal much information to us about what we must shed. At the end of the road, we will walk up the Seven Steps, each one removing the layers of what no longer serves us. The guide will be there every step of the way, but we must choose to climb each step. At the top of the staircase, we will be reduced to our very essence. From here, our guide will weave our true self from our bones and spirit. When this is complete, the guide will lead us through the cave of rebirth back into our physical bodies.

This is a complex journey. I've included guidelines for processing it after the text.

Preparation: purification of body, mind and space is essential for the success of this journey. You should arrange a space in which you can lie down comfortably for an extended period of time. Note that you shouldn't attempt this journey without completing the prior six steps. They have prepared you for it. Skipping ahead to it without doing them will lead to disastrous results. Note that this journey should not be attempted if you are experiencing current significant health problems that interfere with the usual activities of daily living. If you are wound up even after preparation, do The True Magic Meditation first.

If possible, this journey should be done during the first evening of the Full Moon. You may be quite disoriented afterwards. It is important to be very gentle with yourself as you process the journey, especially for the first 24 hours after. I don't recommend going from this journey to the initiation ritual directly. You can do that up to a week after this journey. Take your time during this process.

You should be covered while doing the journey. If you are

comfortable, be naked under the blankets. If not, white is a suitable color to wear. You can also wear white after the journey to symbolize your unity. White is the color of the journey.

Arrange the myrrh, elm and moonstone beside your space. Shamanic or chanting music can be listened to, such as those I've previously mentioned.

Ascended Spirit Guides

The type of spirit guide you'll receive along The Starry Road is that of an ascended master. This entity can take many forms, from human to pure energy. These beings can take on many different forms - from human to animal to purely energetic. Whatever it is they are in the original form, how we perceive them as humans is filtered through our own personality and experiences. Spirit guides are a type of witch's companion, although non-witches can have them, too. The guide you meet on this journey may become your long-term companion or present solely for the rebirth process.

Each step on the Starry Road stairway represents the steps behind you. As you walk up them, feel the energy of all you've accomplished cleansing you. Freeing you. Bringing rebirth into you complete True Self. The Mighty Witch you are.

Beginning the Journey

Get comfortable. Close your eyes. Activate your imagination now. Set the intention to go where the imagery takes you. Do not resist any images or experiences. You'll be protected and completely safe. When the journey is over, you'll return from the meditative state to normal waking calm and refreshed. You'll feel strong and confident, and fully supported by your new guide.

Journey Script

Begin to feel the weight of your body sink in the bed or floor beneath you. Feel the weight in your feet and ankles shift to the floor, now the weight shifts up your calves, then your knees, your legs. Take a moment to feel how heavy they are underneath...... this is a pleasant sensation of heaviness...like being under blankets...warm and soothing....

Now shift your attention to your torso. Feel your butt grow heavy, your lower back.............up your spine as all the weight of your organs is released into your back....your body is deeply relaxed...

Let the back of your arms accept the weight from the front.... heavy, warm, relaxed, comfortable...pull the feeling into the back of your neck.......the back of your head......

Pause here to feel how light the front of your body has become...notice that all tension has been released......start at your head...now clear of thoughts and stress....your face is relaxed...smile a bit....your throat is soft...your breath relaxed and easy...................

Your heart rate is slowing....your belly calm......your legs are at rest.....as are your ankles and feet....warm, relaxed, comfortable....

Now let the weight in your feet melt into the bed or floor beneath you....do the same for your ankles....calves....knees.... legs.....

Pause here to enjoy their lightness....no pain, tension, just relaxed....

Do the same for your back....release all the heaviness in your back into the bed or floor beneath you....

Feel the lightness as it moves through your body....

Now move onto your arms....release the weight into the bed or floor....the neck follows...then your head......

Your feel light, calm, relaxed, comfortable....

Envision all this weight travelling down through the bed or floor, down into the earth...all tension, worries and cares goes along...thank the earth for accepting the heaviness....

In this state of lightness, allow your souls to open. The energy of your spirit, the Three Souls combined, is made entirely of stardust. This energy permeates your every cell, calling you upward to The Starry Road. You are now in a state of unity: the lightness and strength of the stardust fills you completely. All heaviness, all fear is long gone.

Your energetic body is pulled upward, called home by the stars you are made of. The Starry Road awaits. You travel up through the earth's atmosphere, past the Full Moon. You land at the entrance to The Starry Road. Your feet are treading on star dust. The full moon is behind you. You step boldly onto the road. The feeling is of complete unity with the stars, the universe and beyond. The energy is intense, but all that you don't need passes through you effortlessly.

Notice the appearance of The Starry Road for later processing. When you are ready, call upon your guide to come forward.

I ask you, great guide, to help me through rebirth.
So that I may live as my true self
That I may live a magical life and be in unity.
Out of great respect, I call upon you, Great Guide, to guide me on my journey.

Your guide is coming towards you. Greet the guide, take in their physical being. File away their name and their appearance for reflection after the journey. At this point, your guide will deliver a message to you and give you the name you are to call them. Listen patiently.

Call to them using this name. Say that you are ready to follow them to the Seven Steps of Rebirth.

The guide beckons you to follow.

Walk with the guide...let the images flow....

As you approach the stairs, your white star dust cloak evaporates. Stand naked before the steps. Climb the first stair.

Rest here. Envision your past hurts and pain flaking off you. You are shedding your false skin. Your guide remains by your side. You are safe. As the skin is shed, you begin to feel healing.

On the second step, you release the weight of judgment and criticism by others. This tension is removed as your false tissue falls away. Feel the lightness as this is removed. Your guide remains by your side. You are safe.

The third step will cleanse you further of your false identity. The fatty layer of self-blame, self-judgment and self-harm is gone. Your being is further lightened. Your guide remains by your side. You are safe.

On the fourth step you shed all fears about your personal power. The hidden anxieties about standing true are released from your muscles. Relieved of these burdens, you experience greater lightness. Your guide remains by your side. You are safe.

The fifth step is the release of all embedded pain in your deepest places, represented by the organs. Feel the cleansing of them as they shed their false form. Your guide remains by your side. You are safe.

On the sixth step, the toxicity within your bones is banished. The beginnings of unity stir in your freed spirit. Your guide remains by your side. You are safe.

The final step is the purification of your spirit, the Three Souls. All that doesn't serve is released. Your guide remains by your side. You are safe.

When you are reduced to your pure energy form, your guide leads you to a white platform. Lie your energetic being on this. As you lie there, your guide weaves your unified true self, beginning with your Three Selves, then your bones, organs, muscles, tissue and skin. A sense of unity and truth permeates this true form. You are reborn into your True Self. Remain here until you are ready to return to your physical body.

When you are ready, indicate so to your guide. They lead you to a beautiful dark cave.

Enter the cave with the guide. Walk through the cave. As you do, your guide will slowly begin to detach. At the exit to the cave, you return fully to your physical being. Breathe deeply, feeling the strength and wisdom, retaining the lightness.

Now that you are back in your body, in everyday life, take time to notice any physical sensations that are occurring. Note these as well. Activation of certain body parts or systems after a journey shows us further information for healing.

Take time to reflect upon your journey. When you are ready, open your eyes.

Processing Your Rebirth

As soon as possible after the journey, journal about it. Spirit guides often speak to us in riddles and symbols. Writing about them can help us unravel their meanings. Remember that this is very intense. Take time to process.

1. Record immediately all the details of the journey that you remember. Using the voice memo function on your phone is a great tool for doing this or summarize the journey in your journal.

2. Processing the journey should occur soon after, but can wait until later, especially if you made a recording.

Prompts for processing:

- What is my current emotional state? (You'll carry the dominant feelings of the journey over into the mundane world.)
- What physical sensations am I experiencing? (Your body will feel different.)
- What did The Starry Road look like?
- What did my spirit guide look like?
- What did they say to me?
- What did I say?
- What memories do I have of the Seven Steps?

- What did my guide say as they wove me anew?
- What images did I see while they were weaving my True Self?
- What did I experience in the cave?

3. Interpretation: Now that you've processed the journey, you should move on to your interpretation of it. You should start with your understanding, write it down and then seek other sources, such as a standard journey interpretation guide and references on the type of spirit guide (e.g., animal medicine, angelic types, more info on the deity if that's who your guide is).

4. Follow up:

- Be gentle with yourself for the day after the journey experience. The emotions of the journey may carry forward into your waking life. Take time to notice these feelings and release them if they don't serve you well.
- Pay attention for further messages from your guide in your dreams, symbols and other messages that reinforce your connection with them during the days afterwards.
- Return to the cave when you wish to communicate with your guide.
- Arrange a tribute to your guide with symbols and images associated with them as part of your altar or in a separate space.

You complete your altar after the initiation on the next few pages...

Further Reading

Books

Joseph Campbell, *Pathways to Bliss: Mythology and Personal Transformation*

Clare Goodrick-Clarke, *Alchemical Medicine for the 21st Century*

Elizabeth Gilbert, *Big Magic: Creative Living Beyond Fear*

Jon Kabat-Zinn, *Full Catastrophe Living (Revised Edition): Using the Wisdom of Your Body and Mind to Face Stress, Pain, and Illness*

Christopher Penczak, *Ascension Magic*

Rupert Spira, *The Nature of Consciousness: Essays on the Unity of Mind and Matter*

The Kybalion by Three Initiates explains the Hermetic Principles that greatly inform True Magic. You can read it here: http://www.sacred-texts.com/eso/kyb/index.htm

Blogs

Esoteric Online, *Alchemy Step 1 – Basic Principles*. Available at: http://www.esotericonline.net/group/alchemy/page/alchemy-step-1-basic-principles

Cyndi Brannen, *So Long, Uncle Lucky: Saying Goodbye to Spirit Guides*. Available at: http://www.patheos.com/blogs/keepingherkeys/2018/01/goodbye-spirit-guides/

Cyndi Brannen, *Where I Fear to Tread: Angels and Witchcraft*. Available at: http://www.patheos.com/blogs/keepingherkeys/2018/01/im-afraid-of-angels/

Colton Swabb, *The Hermetic Revival: 7 Ancient Principles For Self-Mastery*. Available at: https://medium.com/the-mission/the-hermetic-revival-7-ancient-principles-for-self-mastery-9399e523648d

True Magic Initiation

Initiation is another form of rebirth. I recommend that you wait a few days after doing the rebirth journey before doing the initiation. However, you can work on the other parts of the self-initiation process before the rebirth journey and the initiation ritual. Do the Self-Evaluation once you've completed everything in this step except for the journey and the initiation process. I suggest doing this before you make your Talisman because it will prime your memories about all that you've learned and how you are creating your magical life, then move onto the Cingulum crafting. Once these activities are completed you are well prepared for your True Magic Initiation.

Self-Evaluation

The self-evaluation can be found in the Appendix. Do the evaluation using the steps and your notes. However, you should begin the test without consulting either source. Do as much as you can without it. The areas where you need to use the resources to complete should be noted for further study after initiation. This is a test, but not the pass/fail kind. The goal is to complete it in such a way that you can refer to it as a reference for the key concepts of True Magic.

Making Your Talisman

You'll consecrate your talisman during the initiation ritual. The talisman should include the seven colors. Beyond this you can include replicas of the tools, stones and the botanicals used, planetary symbols and more. Select seven areas of your magical life you're creating that correspond to each of the colors/steps. Use your magical life spell as a reference. Craft using polymer clay, wood or another durable substance a charm for each one. As you create each charm, focus on your intention for it. Envision it coming true. Allow yourself to experience the emotions associated with it. See yourself doing the actions of it.

Connect each one to a cord. Don't assemble the talisman because you'll do so during the initiation ritual. Keep these charms and the other parts of your talisman in a dark colored bag and store on a windowsill or on a plate of salt. If you have extra stones from the steps, you can place them in the bag. The goal is to charge the charms. After the ritual, you'll carry the talisman with you to help attune it to your energy AND as a reminder of the magical life you're creating AND all the work you've done to get to this place.

The inspiration for this talisman is my own personal one that I made three years ago. It was a time of great transformation for me. I felt completely stuck. The talisman I created went into my personal commitment ritual for creating a magical life. I've achieved everything that I put into that talisman. I still keep it near my desk as a reminder that: 1. Magic works, and 2. Believe in the impossible. I worked my butt off, too. Magic works for those who hustle.

Crafting a Cingulum

Traditionally this is a belt, although I wear mine as a bracelet. Choose whichever is most comfortable for you. This is a braided cord consisting of the colors of a tradition. You can add a septagram at the end of the cord. This can be made in advance and stored with your charm. During the ritual, it is placed on the altar until the time comes to put it on. You can also purchase a bracelet or necklace to wear. The cingulum is worn only during witchcraft.

Planning Your Initiation Ceremony

The ceremony includes completing the septagram altar. You can arrange it with the candles, tools, botanicals and stones used throughout the Steps. The altar represents your accomplishment and honors the elements and worlds. For the censer, choose the incense that you are most connected to. Myrrh, mugwort and sage are all suitable for this working. You should wear black for the initiation ceremony. The standard purification of mind, body and space procedures should be follower. Cast the Circle of Seven.

Declaration of Initiation

Your Declaration of Initiation is the statement that you read during the Initiation Ceremony. There is a basic script provided below that you can use, or you can embellish it how you feel led. You can add your personal words of power as you feel led. What's important is that you write a statement that confirms your commitment to the steps of and creating your magical life. Although you are free to add to the declaration, I urge you to keep it simple. You should copy it into your Book of Shadows with the other specifics about the Ceremony (date, offerings, etc.) in advance.

Ceremony

Have your altar, censer, talisman and cingulum ready in your space as well as any offerings you'll be making. Begin by Casting the Circle of Seven, then move into the Declaration of Initiation.

Stand before your septagram altar. Light your chosen incense.

Raise your hands to the Full Moon, lifting the censer high. Then say:

On this night of the Full Moon,
I claim my True Magic.
To the Worlds and Elements, hear me now.
To the planets, plants and stones, I speak these words.
From my selves and souls and the unified whole that I am,
I choose this path.

Arms stay raised. Say:

I claim my unity,
And the powers of the Upper World,
Realm of Intellect and my Higher Self.

Place the censer on the altar.
Anoint the unity charm with the oil and your crown
Light the unity candle
Arms in front, palms down. Say:

I claim my abundance,
And the powers of the Element of Earth,
Blessings of the material world flow to me.

Anoint the abundance charm with the oil and your forehead.
Light the abundance candle
Fingers touching throat. Say:

I claim my connection to all
That is, was and ever will be,
And the powers of the Middle World,
Realm of Action and my Middle Self.

Anoint the connection charm with the oil and your throat.
Light the connection candle
Fingers touching heart center. Say:

I claim my inner flame fueling my growth,
And the spiral that is the Element of Fire,
The powers of creation and destruction are mine.

Anoint the growth charm with the oil and your heart center.
Light the growth candle

Fingers touching just below the solar plexus. Say:

I claim my sovereignty,
My mighty witch powers unleashed
Within and without.

Anoint the sovereignty charm with the oil and just below your
solar plexus.
    Light the sovereignty candle
    Fingers touching belly button. Say:

I claim my boundaries and relationships,
And the Element of Air,
The energy of wind and my breath.
Anoint the energy charm and your belly button.

Light the energy candle
    Hands down. Say:

I claim my healing,
And the depths of the Under World, my Lower Self,
And the Element of Water,
The energy of emotions.

Anoint the healing charm and the lower abdomen.
    Light the healing candle
    Tie the seven charms together. Then say:

To the Worlds and Elements,
Receive my gratitude for your powers lent,
To the Moon, know my thankfulness.
Through your powers and that of the planets,
plants and stones,
And my might,

I am reborn this night.

Pass the cingulum through the smoke several times. Put on the cingulum.

Out of perfect love and perfect trust,
As within, so without.
As above, so below.
So speak I and it is SO!

Extinguish the flames.

Spend as much time here as you wish. Your guide may appear at this point. Invite them into the circle if you choose. When ready, open the circle.

This ritual will be quite energizing. Take time to process the ritual, capitalizing on the abundant energy following through you. Release any excess as desired.

Congratulations! You are now initiated into True Magic! You've claimed your power!

Living True Magic

Now is the real beginning. Such an exciting time. Continue with your Witches' Hour of Power practice. Mix it up to keep growing. I'm offering you the Magic Seven Tarot Spread and a list of ways to practical wild witchery as gifts for unleashing your Inner Witch. Living your truth as a sovereign witch is an amazing lifestyle. Keep developing your skills, working on your Magical Life Project and being grateful.

The Magic Seven Tarot Spread

This reading should be performed at the beginning of each lunar cycle to help you plan for the month ahead. Concentrate on each principle as your shuffle the cards for each draw. Consider the meaning of each card on its own and within the unified whole of the reading. Arrange the cards in the shape of the septagram. Each card will provide guidance for each step: #1: healing, #2, relationships, #3 sovereignty, #4 growth, #5 connecting, #6 abundance and #7 wholeness.

Wild Witchcraft Tips and Practices

Use bodily fluids in spells and rituals. If you are a menstruating female, figure out a way that's right for you to include this monthly ingredient.

Go on a quest for spell ingredients, a new wand or something else. I often set an intention - or get an intuitive feeling - before going on a hike about a certain event or object that will come forward while I'm exploring.

Encounter animals, especially your totems or familiars, in their natural habitat. Birds are everywhere. Sit in the park practicing shape shifting into your favorite local species. Crows are an obvious choice.

Grow plants in your own home, maybe even risky ones like

a poison. (Keep away from children and all the other safety procedures. Don't touch that aconite with your bare hands - voice of experience speaking here.)

Challenge your physical self. I think that the witches' middle world self can get incredibly restless when we spend too much time in our heads. Witch it up by setting intentions or making it into a "correspondence quest."

Study a Wild Goddess, such as Artemis, that island-bound ultimate Wild Witch, Kirke {HYPERLINK "http://www.patheos.com/blogs/keepingherkeys/2018/07/kirke-the-original-witch-her-story-themes-correspondences-and-more/"} or the indomitable Medea {HYPERLINK http://www.patheos.com/blogs/keepingherkeys/2018/06/medea-the-eternal-witch/}

Connect with your witch ancestors through research and trance work.

You are so ready for your magical life. All my blessings for your journey.

Living a life of fierce love, passion and emotional courage is True Magic.
Wild and true.
It is you.

Preparing and Using Tarot Cards

Tarot cards reflect an individual's personal energy signature first and foremost. They are a way of accessing knowledge that may be blocked from our conscious mind due to stress, the shadow self or other reasons. The cards connect with our Higher Self and our Guardians (known and unknown). Guardians can be ancestors, deities and all manner of entities.

The Cards can be used for divination or for personal development. My preference is always for the latter, although insight into potential outcomes is helpful at times.

The Cards offer wisdom, reflection and guidance. Nothing in the Cards is preordained. Free will, our ability to heal the past, control our present, and embrace our future, is always the dominant force in any sort of spiritual work, including working with the Cards.

The Cards, however, do offer great truth as they reflect the energy we project onto them. If the cards in your spread cause you discomfort, or if their message is not immediately clear, spend some time reflecting on why this is. Always honor the information presented by the Cards. Always be grateful for their power to heal.

Thank your guides, your Divine Source, and the divine energy within when you work with the Cards. Do this at the beginning of your self-reading and at the close.

As you heal, you may wish to carry a card or two with you to remind you of what you are working on. You can also keep those cards near your bedside for meditation in the morning and/or upon retiring for the day.

Preparing your Deck

The Tarot Cards must be prepared prior to use. This note outlines the way I do it, in case you don't have a preferred method.

When you are doing each of the three stages, concentrate on the intention underlying each action. For example, when cleansing, think; "I cleanse this deck of all other energies. It is clear and fresh."

At each step in the preparation process, concentrate on the intention for that step. See examples in each step

Cleansing: I prefer used decks to new. New decks are full of the energy that went into creating them. My personal preference is a worn in deck. I don't recommend this approach for beginners because it can be quite a challenge to cleanse, protect and charge used decks. New is easier for beginners. Regardless of deck origin, cleanse the deck by wrapping in a previously prepared (cleansed, protected, charged) cloth (I always use black, but you can use whatever appeals to you). Place cards in cloth. Immerse deck entirely in salt or earth for at least overnight. If you want to be super technical, I'd do it during the waxing moon because you are removing energies that aren't yours. I keep them outside while this is going on. Place in a window (preferably open) if you can't leave them outside. Once this step is completed, unwrap, discard or wash the cloth. Now, smoke the cards (not literally!) with either sage or a mixture of cleansing herbs. Make sure you get each card in the smoke. Your intention during this stage is "I cleanse these cards of all previous energy. They are fresh and renewed."

Protecting: Use the sage a second time to protect the cards. I also use a clear quartz point; you can use various protective herbs and crystals. Wrap the whole thing up. Store at least overnight. Intention during this stage can be "I protect these cards from any harmful energy. They are secure and pure."

Charging: Remove from the bundle. Discard or wash cloth. Put the cards in your pillow case and sleep with them for at least a week. This is so the cards get to know your personal energy signature. You can carry them with you, too. Prior to first use, do another burn of herbs appropriate to your reading's intention.

Your intention is "I charge these cards for use of my highest good. They reflect pure energy."

Ready for use! Like I wrote earlier, this is just my way. Do it however you like, just do it. They don't work properly without these three steps being followed.

Interpretation

Remember to use both your intuitive interpretation and the standard interpretation for the cards. Your truth will be a combination of these things. Standardized interpretations are available with each deck. Some decks have full books that can also be purchased. There are websites devoted to standard interpretation (I like this one: http://www.aeclectic.net/tarot/learn/meanings/). I have a few lengthy Tarot interpretation books as pdf's if you want to go deeper (including the original Waite interpretation.)

The intuitive interpretation is the immediate thoughts that come to mind when you concentrate your focus on a card. Look at the symbols, images and colors. What do they mean to you?

Each card is energetically linked to the other cards in the reading, especially the ones immediately adjacent. If there is a particularly powerful message coming through, cards can reflect this rather than the being associated with the meaning associated with their "spot" in a spread. Pay attention to trends.

Sometimes the meaning of a card or an entire spread can be difficult to discern. Sit with them. Reflect upon your recorded thoughts and the standardized interpretation. The meaning will reveal itself with focus and, sometimes, time.

Storing Cards

I keep my cards stored wrapped in black cloth with various symbols on it (personal meaning for me). Store the cards safely either in this manner or use a method that makes sense to you.

Reading for Others

If you read for others, I recommend using a separate deck than this personal one. If you use your personal one, you'll need to change the charge of the cards prior to reading for another. Simply let the cards know that you are removing your personal energy signal from there to help another heal. When you are done your reading, recharge your cards for your personal use.

Quiz

1. Discuss "a lot of magic is about alleviating distress."
2. Describe the properties of yarrow that are suitable for healing.
3. Compare and contrast removal and reversal magic.
4. What does it mean to be an ethical witch?
5. Discuss the properties of the element of air.
6. What are the Seven Witches' Principles?
7. Provide an example of great short incantation.
8. Describe the process and experience of self-anointing.
9. The color red is associated with both the Full Moon and the crossroads. Discuss how they have similar energies.
10. What are the magical properties of orange peel?
11. Comment on your experience with The Spell of the Seven Fires.
12. How can the feather be used as a magical tool?
13. Describe your experiences using hand signals to call upon the seven energies.
14. How have you used your personal Words of Power?
15. Do you make offerings to the energies, entities and deities that you associate with? Why or why not?
16. How are you creating your magical life?
17. Discuss your personal experience working with myrrh.
18. How do you "own" your witchery?
19. Briefly describe your understanding of the progression from healing to wholeness.
20. How has The Witches' Hour of Power changed your life?
21. What's next on your Witches' Journey?

**MOON
BOOKS**

PAGANISM & SHAMANISM

What is Paganism? A religion, a spirituality, an alternative belief system, nature worship? You can find support for all these definitions (and many more) in dictionaries, encyclopaedias, and text books of religion, but subscribe to any one and the truth will evade you. Above all Paganism is a creative pursuit, an encounter with reality, an exploration of meaning and an expression of the soul. Druids, Heathens, Wiccans and others, all contribute their insights and literary riches to the Pagan tradition. Moon Books invites you to begin or to deepen your own encounter, right here, right now.

If you have enjoyed this book, why not tell other readers by posting a review on your preferred book site.

Recent bestsellers from Moon Books are:

Journey to the Dark Goddess
How to Return to Your Soul
Jane Meredith
Discover the powerful secrets of the Dark Goddess and
transform your depression, grief and pain into healing
and integration.
Paperback: 978-1-84694-677-6 ebook: 978-1-78099-223-5

Shamanic Reiki
Expanded Ways of Working with Universal Life Force Energy
Llyn Roberts, Robert Levy
Shamanism and Reiki are each powerful ways of healing; together,
their power multiplies. *Shamanic Reiki* introduces techniques to
help healers and Reiki practitioners tap ancient healing wisdom.
Paperback: 978-1-84694-037-8 ebook: 978-1-84694-650-9

Pagan Portals – The Awen Alone
Walking the Path of the Solitary Druid
Joanna van der Hoeven
An introductory guide for the solitary Druid, *The Awen Alone* will
accompany you as you explore, and seek out your own place
within the natural world.
Paperback: 978-1-78279-547-6 ebook: 978-1-78279-546-9

A Kitchen Witch's World of Magical Herbs & Plants
Rachel Patterson
A journey into the magical world of herbs and plants, filled with
magical uses, folklore, history and practical magic. By popular
writer, blogger and kitchen witch, Tansy Firedragon.
Paperback: 978-1-78279-621-3 ebook: 978-1-78279-620-6

Medicine for the Soul
The Complete Book of Shamanic Healing
Ross Heaven
All you will ever need to know about shamanic healing and how to become your own shaman...
Paperback: 978-1-78099-419-2 ebook: 978-1-78099-420-8

Shaman Pathways – The Druid Shaman
Exploring the Celtic Otherworld
Danu Forest
A practical guide to Celtic shamanism with exercises and techniques as well as traditional lore for exploring the Celtic Otherworld.
Paperback: 978-1-78099-615-8 ebook: 978-1-78099-616-5

Traditional Witchcraft for the Woods and Forests
A Witch's Guide to the Woodland with Guided Meditations and Pathworking
Mélusine Draco
A Witch's guide to walking alone in the woods, with guided meditations and pathworking.
Paperback: 978-1-84694-803-9 ebook: 978-1-84694-804-6

Wild Earth, Wild Soul
A Manual for an Ecstatic Culture
Bill Pfeiffer
Imagine a nature-based culture so alive and so connected, spreading like wildfire. This book is the first flame...
Paperback: 978-1-78099-187-0 ebook: 978-1-78099-188-7

Naming the Goddess
Trevor Greenfield
Naming the Goddess is written by over eighty adherents and
scholars of Goddess and Goddess Spirituality.
Paperback: 978-1-78279-476-9 ebook: 978-1-78279-475-2

Shapeshifting into Higher Consciousness
Heal and Transform Yourself and Our World with Ancient
Shamanic and Modern Methods
Llyn Roberts
Ancient and modern methods that you can use every day to
transform yourself and make a positive difference in the world.
Paperback: 978-1-84694-843-5 ebook: 978-1-84694-844-2

Readers of ebooks can buy or view any of these bestsellers by
clicking on the live link in the title. Most titles are published in
paperback and as an ebook. Paperbacks are available in traditional
bookshops. Both print and ebook formats are available online.

Find more titles and sign up to our readers' newsletter at
http://www.johnhuntpublishing.com/paganism
Follow us on Facebook at https://www.facebook.com/MoonBooks
and Twitter at https://twitter.com/MoonBooksJHP